13 Nov 94

Dear Libby,

As we talked today I could feel the strength of your conversion & testimony — what a wonderful decision to be baptized.

Love God & be obedient — — — then you will find true happiness.

Ted A. Allen

REACH UP
FOR THE LIGHT

REACH UP
FOR THE LIGHT

James E. Faust

Deseret Book Company
Salt Lake City, Utah

This book is not an official publication of The Church of Jesus Christ of Latter-day Saints. It has been prepared by the author, and he alone is responsible for the contents.

© 1990 James E. Faust

Library of Congress Cataloging-in-Publication Data

Faust, James E., 1920–
  Reach up for the light / by James E. Faust.
    p. cm.
  Includes index.
  ISBN 0-87579-418-1
  1. Spiritual life—Mormon authors. I. Title.
BX8656.F378 1990
248.4'89332—dc20   90-38503
                                                               CIP

Printed in the United States of America
10   9   8   7   6   5   4   3   2   1

CONTENTS

I, the Lord, am merciful and gracious unto those who fear me, and delight to honor those who serve me in righteousness and in truth unto the end.

Great shall be their reward and eternal shall be their glory.

And to them will I reveal all mysteries, yea, all the hidden mysteries of my kingdom from days of old, and for ages to come, will I make known unto them the good pleasure of my will concerning all things pertaining to my kingdom.

Yea, even the wonders of eternity shall they know, and things to come will I show them, even the things of many generations.

And their wisdom shall be great, and their understanding reach to heaven.

—D&C 76:5–9

Chapter 1

REACH UP
FOR THE LIGHT

A marvelous vision that Joseph Smith had concerning the Twelve Apostles in his day has profound significance for me. Heber C. Kimball recorded, "The following vision was manifested to him [Joseph Smith] as near as I can recollect:

"He saw the Twelve going forth, and they appeared to be in a far distant land. After some time they unexpectedly met together, apparently in great tribulation, their clothes all ragged, and their knees and feet sore. They formed into a circle, and all stood with their eyes fixed upon the ground. The Savior appeared and stood in their midst and wept over them, and wanted to show Himself to them, but they did not discover Him." (Orson F. Whitney, *Life of Heber C. Kimball,* 2d ed., Salt Lake City: Bookcraft, p. 93.)

A message that can be inferred from this is that because the Twelve had suffered so much, had endured so greatly, and had so exhausted themselves in leading the battle of righteousness, they were bowed down and did not look up. Had they only looked up they might have beheld the Lord Jesus, who wanted them to see him, weeping over them, suffering with them, and standing in their midst.

Some time ago we were in one of the oldest cities on

1

earth. Some of the greatest wonders of the world are there; so are crime, squalor, poverty, and filth. Our kind hosts observed as we were making our way through the teeming masses—past the overloaded donkeys, the filth, the smells—that everything was beautiful in that city if you raised your sights and only looked a foot or more above the ground.

In recent times the prices of oil, gold, and other precious minerals have greatly increased. These treasures are all obtained by looking down. They are useful and necessary, but they are tangible riches. What of the treasures that are to be found by raising our vision? What of the intangible riches that come from the pursuit of holiness? Stephen looked upward. "He, being full of the Holy Ghost, looked up stedfastly into heaven, and saw the glory of God, and Jesus standing on the right hand of God." (Acts 7:55.)

My heart and understanding go out to our young people. They have to cope with a darkness and moral fog as dense as many of us can ever remember. We live in a world where success seems largely measured by possessions. How the possessions may have been acquired often seems immaterial. Honesty, decency, chastity, and holiness are frequently downgraded as being of lesser worth than possessions. Are our young people enticed to look up or down?

The desire for profitable gain and popularity in the entertainment world has unmasked in the most appealing ways all of the evils of the human race. The most revolting practices and perversions have been masqueraded and even urged upon our inexperienced young people by some seeking to seductively merchandise the evil side of human behavior. Consciences seem seared with a hot iron; spiritual cells seem closed. Ideals of emptiness and uselessness of life are fostered. Nobility of thought and purpose seems not to be sufficiently taught, encouraged, or valued.

2

The standard of the common thief—"What can we get away with?"—has become the standard for many in the world rather than what our own integrity ought to demand that we do. What has happened to self-respect and personal integrity, which would not permit even entertaining the idea of doing cheap or small things? An example might be our relationship with the financial credit by which the world's commerce is carried on. Often we forget that those who extend credit to us are also extending trust and confidence in us. Our own integrity is involved. I recall my father speaking with profound respect of a man whom Father as a lawyer had taken through bankruptcy. Given time, this man paid in full all of his creditors who had trusted him and extended confidence in him, even though he was legally relieved of paying the debts. Our own integrity is a substantial part of our individual worth.

How can Christian belief and morality translate more completely into Christian action? Does our commitment fall short of being a consecration? The doubting Thomas wanted to believe; he believed partway. It is my firm persuasion that building self-esteem sufficiently to forsake all evil requires consecration to the saving principles and ordinances of the gospel under divine priesthood authority. It must be consecration to simple, basic Christian principles, including honesty to self and others, forgetting of self, integrity of thought and action. The principles of the restored gospel are so plain, so clear, so compassionate, so endowed with beauty, so graced with love unfeigned, as to be imprinted with the indisputable impress of the Savior himself.

There also need to be a confrontation with and mastery of life's challenges, especially those that come with temptation. Instead of squarely and honestly meeting the problems of life, many negotiate their way through difficulties, ration-

3

alizing their departure from the great truths which bring happiness and justifying the leaving of their sacred promises and holy commitments for seemingly logical but fragile and unjustifiable reasons.

I cannot help wondering if we have not fallen short of the mark. Have we been measuring by standards that are too short and unworthy of those in the pursuit of holiness? Have we taken too much comfort in feeling that we have qualified through our attendance at meetings or through minimal involvement in a conscience-easing effort? Have our guidelines been a ceiling instead of a floor?

Upon returning from living in South America, I was struck by the lack of self-esteem revealed in the manner by which so many people now clothe themselves in public. To attract attention or in the name of comfort and informality, many have sunk not only to immodesty but also to slovenliness. Against their own self-interest, they present themselves to others in the worst possible way.

In forsaking the great principle of modesty, society has paid a price in the violation of a greater but related principle — that of chastity. The purveyors of the concept of irresponsible sexual relations that degrade and brutalize the participants have grossly masqueraded and completely missed the purpose of these divine gifts.

Chastity before marriage and faithfulness after marriage are cardinal ingredients for the full flowering of sacred love between husband and wife. Chastity nurtures and builds feelings of self-worth and indemnifies against the destruction of self-image.

One of the root social problems of our day concerns the lack of self-esteem. A shallow self-image is not reinforced by always letting others establish our standards or by habitually succumbing to peer pressure. Young people too often depend upon someone else's image rather than their own.

Insecurity and lack of self-esteem may be related to lack of self-respect. Can we respect ourselves when we do things that we do not admire and may even condemn in others? Repenting of transgressions and forsaking of weaknesses represent, on the other hand, a great restorative salve for the strengthening of human worth and dignity.

Since virtue and faith too often do not readily trade in the marketplace, some may feel that they can live by whatever standards their whim and fancy suggest. In a value-free society — free of morals, free of standards — many also live free of feelings of self-worth, self-respect, and dignity. Far too many young people, and older ones, too, fail to realize, as the motto of the city of Nottingham, England, affirms: *"Vivet post funera virtus"* ("Virtue lives on after death").

In the intellectual approach to human worth, the values of faith in God and virtuous behavior cannot be quantitatively proven or measured, and so faith and virtue are often rejected by many as worthless. This is a route destined to failure because it does not take into account the powerful importance of the subjective things we can know but not measure. For instance, I love my wife and family and I feel their love for me. You cannot measure how deep our feelings of love are for each other, but that love is very real to us. Pain is also difficult to measure, but it is real. The same is true of faith in God. We can know of his existence without being able to quantitatively measure it. Paul states, "The Spirit itself beareth witness with our spirit, that we are the children of God." (Romans 8:16.)

What are the limits on commitment of the heart of those who pursue holiness? Fortunately, this is a matter for each

5

to decide. We achieve perfection, however, in the doing of many things, and can be perfect in our intent to do all things.

In my opinion, it was not contemplated by the great Creator that man- and womankind are intended to wallow in selfishness and self-gratification. After all, "in the image of God created he him; male and female created he them." (Genesis 1:27.) "What is man, that thou art mindful of him?" asks the Psalmist. "For thou hast made him a little lower than the angels, and hast crowned him with glory and honour. Thou madest him to have dominion over the works of thy hands; thou hast put all things under his feet." (Psalm 8:4–6.)

What is the standard of holiness? The answer comes from the scriptures: "Who is like unto thee, O Lord, . . . glorious in holiness?" (Exodus 15:11.)

Like Stephen, those who pursue holiness see the glory of God. The blessings that shall come in the pursuit of holiness were in part described by the Lord: "Verily, thus saith the Lord: It shall come to pass that every soul who forsaketh his sins and cometh unto me, and calleth on my name, and obeyeth my voice, and keepeth my commandments, shall see my face and know that I am." (D&C 93:1.)

Earlier I referred to the vision of Joseph the Prophet concerning the Twelve Apostles in his time. No one need assume that the Twelve who failed to see the Savior because they stood with their eyes fixed upon the ground had in any way failed in their labors. As a body they continued strong and stedfast in their ministry. Their discouragement was only temporary. Their labors were heroic; their acts were bold and courageous. Joseph the Prophet, at the conclusion of that vision, was privileged to see the completion of the work of the Twelve. Heber C. Kimball records: "He [Joseph] saw until they had accomplished their work, and arrived at the gate of the celestial city; there Father Adam stood and opened the gate to them, and as they entered he embraced them one by one and kissed them. He [Adam] then led them to the throne of God, and then the Savior embraced each one of them and kissed them, and crowned each one of them in the presence of God. . . . The impression this vision left on Brother Joseph's mind was of so acute a nature, that he never could refrain from weeping while rehearsing it." (*Life of Heber C. Kimball*, pp. 93–94.)

The dignity of self is greatly enhanced by looking upward in the search for holiness. Like the giant trees, we should reach up for the light. The most important source of light we can come to know is the gift of the Holy Ghost. It is the source of inner strength and peace.

I have seen human dignity and self-worth expressed eloquently in the lives of the humblest of the humble, in the lives of the poor as well as in the lives of the formally educated and the affluent. The fruits of the search for holiness in their lives have been transparent, expressed through their inner dignity, their feelings of self-respect and personal worth. Shakespeare, speaking through Polonius, reminds us: "This above all: to thine own self be true / And it must follow, as the night the day, / Thou canst not then be false to any man." (*Hamlet*, act 1, sc. 3.)

Much of our self-respect is built by our own hard work, our thrift, and by trying to be independent as far as possible.

May we have a feeling of personal worth and dignity born of the knowledge that each of us is a child of God, and be strengthened by looking upwards in the pursuit of holiness. As we look up, may we be worthy to receive the inspiration that comes constantly from God, which inspiration is sacred, real, and often very private.

Chapter 2

UNWANTED MESSAGES
AND HARD ANSWERS

A fter World War II was over, I was married and wanted to get on with my life. My memorable mission was finished before my military service. I was not anxious to become a student again and go back to the university where I had started some eight years before. My intended course would require another three years of intensive study, discipline, and poverty. With all of this in mind I said to my father, "I don't think I will go back to school. I'll just get a job or start a business and go forward in my life." My father, who had completed law school after World War I as an older student with a wife and three children, said bluntly, "What can you do?"

His response was so brutally honest that it hurt, but I could not ignore it. I went back to the university and completed the course. This frank but well-intentioned message changed my life.

In the time of Jesus, a certain ruler asked the Savior a very significant question and received a hard answer that he did not want to hear. With the hard answer came a great promise. The meaningful question the rich man asked was: "What shall I do to inherit eternal life?"

Jesus answered, "Thou knowest the commandments, Do

not commit adultery, Do not kill, Do not steal, Do not bear false witness, Honour thy father and thy mother."

And the ruler answered, "All these have I kept from my youth up."

The unwelcome answer then came from the Master: "Yet lackest thou one thing: sell all that thou hast, and distribute unto the poor, and thou shalt have treasure in heaven: and come, follow me."

When the ruler heard this, "he was very sorrowful: for he was very rich." Seeing this, Jesus said, "How hardly shall they that have riches enter into the kingdom of God!" (Luke 18:18, 20–24.)

How people handle their earthly riches is among the greatest tests they have in life.

This same Jesus of Nazareth spoke much novel doctrine that seemed hard to accept. Some said, "What new doctrine is this?" (Mark 1:27.) Jesus did not speak of revenge or of getting even. He spoke of loving our enemies and doing good to those who hate us, of blessing those who curse us, and of praying for those who despitefully use us. He counseled his followers, when smitten on one cheek, to "offer also the other; and him that taketh away thy cloke forbid [him] not to take thy coat also." (Luke 6:27–29.)

Other interesting new doctrines taught by Jesus were to go beyond loving only our own, beyond being good just to our friends, and to lend goods and money without hoping for something in return. He counseled us to be merciful, to be kind to the unthankful and to the evil, and to judge not and condemn not. (See Luke 6:34–37.) And he spoke of being careful "when all men shall speak well of you," because all men spoke well of the false prophets. (Luke 6:26.)

The promise for those who can do these things is great: "Ye shall be the children of the Highest." (Luke 6:35.)

May I mention two or three other messages that seem no longer popular? One is to respect the Sabbath day. While the Savior himself cautioned against extreme forms of Sabbath day observance, it is well to remember whose day the Sabbath is. It seems to be increasingly popular to disregard the commandment to observe and respect the Sabbath day. For many the Sabbath has become a holiday rather than a holy day of rest and sanctification. For some it is a day to shop and buy groceries. The decision of those who engage in shopping, sports, work, and recreation on the Sabbath day is their own, for which they alone bear responsibility.

The Lord's commandment given on Mount Sinai about observing the Sabbath day has not been altered, nor has the Church's affirmation of this commandment. Those who violate it in the exercise of their agency are answerable for losing the blessings that observance would bring. The Lord has spoken in our day concerning the Sabbath day. We are to keep ourselves "unspotted from the world" and to "go to the house of prayer." We are to rest from our labors and pay our devotions "unto the Most High." (D&C 59:9–10.) The Doctrine and Covenants reminds us: "On this day thou shalt do none other thing, only let thy food be prepared with singleness of heart that thy fasting may be perfect, or, in other words, that thy joy may be full." (D&C 59:13.) The blessings for those who do righteousness are supernal. They shall enjoy "peace in this world, and eternal life in the world to come." (D&C 59:23.)

Another transcendent but often unheeded message that peals down from Sinai is "Honour thy father and thy mother." (Exodus 20:12.) I have frequently walked by a rest home that provides excellent care. But it is heartrending to see so many parents and grandparents in that good care facility who are so forgotten, so bereft of dignity, so starved for love. To honor

10

parents certainly means to take care of physical needs. But it means much, much more. It means to show love, kindness, thoughtfulness, and concern for them all the days of their lives. It means to help them preserve their dignity and self-respect in their declining years. It means to honor their wishes and desires and their teachings both before and after they are dead.

Some years ago I created a stake on one of the islands in Japan. As usual, we held many interviews with the leaders to become acquainted with them. One of the men had moved to that area from Tokyo to take care of his aged and ailing father and his father's business, which was in difficulty because of the father's ill health. After the father died, the son went to his father's creditors and acknowledged his father's debts. He requested time from those creditors so that he could assume and pay all of his father's outstanding obligations. In our interview I asked him how he was managing to meet this responsibility. He answered that he was getting along quite well and that he would be able to handle his father's debts. The Lord saw fit to call him to be one of the leaders of that stake.

Besides being one of God's commandments, the kind, thoughtful consideration of parents is a matter of common decency and self-respect. And on their part, parents need to live so as to be worthy of the respect of their children. I cannot help wondering about parents who adopt the attitude with their children, "Do as I say, not as I do," with respect to using harmful substances, going to inappropriate movies, and other questionable activities. Children often take license from their parents' behavior and go beyond the values the parents wish to establish. There is one safe parental rule: do not just avoid evil, avoid the very appearance of evil. (See 1 Thessalonians 5:22.)

11

I should like to speak of one more strong message. It is frequently astounding to see the dereliction of people in keeping the standards of ordinary fairness and justice. This delinquency manifests itself in many ways. It is evident in commercial transactions as well as in private contacts. Injustice to others is manifest even in the way automobiles are sometimes driven. Such unfairness and injustice result principally from one person seeking an advantage or an edge over another. Those who follow such practices demean themselves greatly. How can those who do not practice ordinary fairness and justice have serious claim on the blessings of a just and fair God?

Do some seek to justify their taking of shortcuts and advantage of others by indulging in the twin sophistries, "There isn't any justice" and "Everybody does it"? Many others seemingly prosper by violating the rules of God and the standards of decency and fair play. They appear to escape the imminent law of the harvest, which states, "Whatsoever a man soweth, that shall he also reap." (Galatians 6:7.) Worrying about the punishment we think ought to come to others is self-defeating to us. Brigham Young counseled that unless we ourselves are prepared for the day of the Lord's vengeance when the wicked will be consumed, we should not be too anxious for the Lord to hasten his work. Rather, said he, "let our anxiety be centered upon this one thing, the purifying of our own affections." (*Journal of Discourses* 9:3.)

Many modern professors of human behavior advocate as a cure to an afflicted conscience that we simply ignore the unwanted messages. They suggest that we change the standard to fit the circumstances so that there is no longer a conflict, thus easing the conscience. Those who follow the divine Christ cannot with impunity subscribe to this evil and perverse philosophy. For the troubled conscience in conflict with right and wrong, the only permanent help is to change the behavior and follow a repentant path. The prophet Isaiah taught, "Woe unto them that call evil good, and good evil; that put darkness for light, and light for darkness; that put bitter for sweet, and sweet for bitter!" (Isaiah 5:20.)

During all my ministry, I have been fascinated by the manner in which Jesus hardened the bone and spirit of his chief apostle, Peter. When he told Peter that he had prayed that Peter's faith would strengthen, Peter affirmed that he would go with the Savior to prison or to death. Jesus then said, "Peter, the cock shall not crow this day, before that thou shalt thrice deny that thou knowest me." (Luke 22:34.) After the predicted three denials, the powerful, unwelcome, but steel-hardening message came: Peter heard the cock crow. And he "went out and wept bitterly" (Matthew 26:75), but he was strengthened to fulfill his calling and to die for the cause.

There is one unerring voice that is ever true. It can always be relied upon. It should be listened to, although at times this voice too may speak unwelcome warning messages. I speak of the still, small, inner voice that comes from the divine source. As the prophet Elijah learned, "The Lord was not in the wind: and after the wind an earthquake; but the Lord was not in the earthquake: and after the earthquake a fire; but the Lord was not in the fire: and after the fire a still small voice." (1 Kings 19:11–12.)

One single unwanted message may be a call to change our lives; it may lead to the specially tailored opportunity we need. I am grateful that it is never too late to change, to make things right, to leave old activities and habits behind.

13

Chapter 3

A SIMPLE,
UNTROUBLED FAITH

everal months ago, Elder and Sister F. Arthur Kay and I visited the beautiful, exotic island of Tahiti. Our flight arrived at the Papeete airport at about four in the morning. We were met at the airport by a group of local Church leaders headed by regional representative Victor Cave. We quickly assembled our bags and headed for the hotel to get what rest we could before the day's activities began.

Our route took us through the deserted, dimly lit streets of Papeete. In the dark, we saw the faint figure of a man crossing the street in front of Brother Cave's car. Brother Cave gave the man a lot of room to cross and told us, "That man is Brother So-and-so. He is hurrying to get to the temple. The first session of the temple doesn't begin until nine o'clock, but he wants to be there well in advance."

"How far away does he live?" asked Elder Kay. The answer: "Two or three blocks." Brother Cave indicated that the caretakers open the temple gates early and that this man comes in and watches the day begin within the sacred precincts of the beautiful temple in Papeete.

I marveled at the faith of that man, who was willing to forgo his sleep and other activities in order to meditate and contemplate. Some would no doubt say, "How foolish! How wasteful of time that could be spent sleeping or studying." I choose to hope that in those programmed hours of meditation and contemplation that faithful man was coming to know himself and his Creator.

It is important for us to nurture such a simple, untroubled faith. I urge you not to be unduly concerned about the intricacies, the complexities, and any seeming contradictions that seem to trouble many of us. Sometimes we spend time satisfying our intellectual egos and trying to find all the answers before we accept any.

We are all in pursuit of truth and knowledge. The nurturing of simple, untroubled faith does not limit us in the pursuit of growth and accomplishment. On the contrary, it may intensify and hasten our progress. This is so because our natural gifts and powers of achievement are increasingly enhanced by the endless growth of knowledge. In our belief, it is possible to be even a helper of the Father and of the Son and to be under their personal tutelage.

Nephi explained that his brethren had become "past feeling," even though they had seen and heard an angel, and even though God had spoken to them in a still, small voice. (1 Nephi 17:45.) In contrast, Nephi tells us, "Feast upon the words of Christ; for behold, the words of Christ will tell you all things what ye should do." (2 Nephi 32:3.)

I have a dear friend with whom I grew up. Although bright and able, he was not a scholar. The press of family needs and concerns limited his educational opportunities, and he did not graduate from high school. He acquired an old, beat-up truck and began hauling sand and gravel for a few contractors. The work was seasonal and not at all productive. The old truck frequently broke down and needed repairs. In his teenage years he drifted some, but he married a good woman and settled down. Their circumstances were economically straitened, but somehow they managed to get a house built on part of the family property.

I was the bishop and called this good man to be the Aaronic Priesthood adviser. He took his calling seriously. He literally wore out the handbook, studying it. He had a notebook filled with dates when all the young men in the ward would reach the age to be advanced in the Aaronic Priesthood. He kept good track of the young men and kept the bishopric informed of their activities. Some years after I was released, he became a member of our bishopric. He needed a little nudging to become a full tithe payer, but he responded faithfully, as he had done before. Subsequently, he became our bishop. He served wonderfully and well.

In the meantime, he and an associate had learned how to lay bricks and had formed a brick-contracting partnership. The difference between their work and the work of others was in the quality. He prospered and became well respected in the community. He also became the president of the local water company. And after many successful years as a bishop, he was called to the high council and served well and faithfully. Although his formal education ended before high school graduation, he is now a man of affairs, respected and honored. With the advantage of a college education he no doubt would have achieved even more.

What caused him to succeed? Industry? thrift? self-reliance? Yes, but there was more. Conscientiously and untiringly, he sought to know and do the mind and the will of the Lord. He had a simple, untroubled faith.

Our religion promises the opportunity to come back into the presence of the Father and the Son, and it contemplates a future perfection of the human spirit and soul. This is a preferential condition in the hereafter. Why, then, should we be preoccupied unnecessarily with too many mysteries? In fact, the worldwide mission of the Church can be simply stated; it is to perfect the Saints, proclaim the gospel, and redeem the dead in order to bring God's children to Christ.

President Stephen L Richards explained it this way: "The immortal soul which is the union of body and spirit, becomes invested with divine nature of our eternal Father and our elder Brother, Jesus Christ." (Conference Report, April 1945, p. 30.) That investment of the divine nature intensifies and magnifies our gifts and abilities. There is no greater teacher, no greater strength than the divine nature of the Eternal Father and Jesus Christ.

Our prophets and other Church leaders are also great teachers. Before I was called as a General Authority and had a seat in general conference, I always tried to listen, either by televison or radio, to the conference proceedings. One Saturday of general conference, on the opening day of duck-hunting season, my youngest son and I went duck hunting. Of course, we listened to the car radio on the way and took a portable radio with us so that we could listen to it in the duck blind. The season's shooting began at noon, so we were able to hear the morning's proceedings.

My son had a seminary assignment to review the conference messages. We listened faithfully to all of the messages on Saturday morning. The shooting was over by one o'clock, and we listened to the afternoon's conference proceedings. As we were picking up our decoys and heading back to the car, my son thoughtfully asked, "What are the Brethren saying?" He was trying to understand the grand overarching and undergirding messages of their talks.

We should ask ourselves: What are the Brethren saying? The living prophets can open the visions of eternity; they give counsel on how to overcome the world. We cannot know what that counsel is if we do not listen. We cannot receive the blessings we are promised if we do not follow the counsel given.

As a young stake president, I met many of the General Authorities when they came to speak at our stake conferences. That was a great experience! President Hugh B. Brown, as an Assistant to the Twelve, came to one of our stake conferences just a week before he was sustained as a member of the Council of the Twelve. We enjoyed his warm spirit and his good humor. As I helped him with his coat and walked out to his car with him, I asked, "Elder Brown, do you have any personal advice for me?" "Yes. Stick with the Brethren." He did not choose to elaborate or explain, but he left that indelible message: Have the simple faith to follow the Brethren.

My grandmother, Maud Wetzel Faust, used to tell her young grandsons about going to general conference when President Brigham Young presided. With the exception of the Prophet Joseph Smith, she had known all of the presidents of the Church, up to Heber J. Grant. From her observations over the years, she had this to say: "Those who have turned their backs on the Brethren have not prospered." Then she proceeded to tell of a few examples. What caused her to impart this lesson to her grandsons I do not know, but I would certainly wish all of us would have the simple faith to "stick with the Brethren."

We acknowledge that all Church leaders, past and present—except Christ himself—had human failings and weaknesses. Critics of the Church are wont to discredit this marvelous work because of the human weaknesses of its leaders. But, as President Gordon B. Hinckley said a few years ago, "to highlight the mistakes and gloss over the greater good is to draw a caricature. Caricatures are amusing, but they are often ugly and dishonest. A man may have a wart on his cheek and still have a face of beauty and strength, but if the wart is emphasized unduly in relation to his other features, the portrait is often lacking in integrity." Of the early leaders of the Church, President Hinckley said, "If some of them stumbled, or if their characters may have been slightly flawed in one way or another, the wonder is the greater that they accomplished so much." (*Church News*, July 3, 1983, p. 11.) The same is true today.

In an urgent plea for the Saints to concern themselves more with the common things, President Wilford Woodruff gave this counsel: "How much longer I shall talk to this people I do not know; but I want to say this to all Israel: Cease troubling yourselves about who God is; who Adam is, who Christ is, who Jehovah is. For heaven's sake, let these things alone. Why trouble yourselves about these things? God has revealed himself, and when the 121st section of the Doctrine and Covenants is fulfilled, whether there be one God or many gods they will be revealed to the children of men, as well as all thrones and dominions, principalities, and powers. Then why trouble yourselves about these things? God is God. Christ is Christ. The Holy Ghost is the Holy Ghost. That should be enough for you and me to know. If we want to know any more, wait till we get where God is in person. I say this because we are troubled every little while with inquiries from elders anxious to know who God is, who Christ is, and who Adam is. I say to the elders of Israel, stop this. Humble yourselves before the Lord; seek for light, for truth, and for a knowledge of the common things of the kingdom of God." (*The Discourses of Wilford Woodruff*, ed. G. Homer Durham, Salt Lake City: Bookcraft, 1946, pp. 235–36.)

To have a simple, untroubled faith, we must keep our spiritual innocence. This requires avoiding cynicism and criticism. This is the day of the cynics, the critics, and the pickle-suckers. Said President Hinckley: "Criticism is the forerunner of divorce, the cultivator of rebellion, sometimes a catalyst that leads to failure. In the Church, it sows the seeds of inactivity and finally apostasy."

For some years I shared a common reception room at the Church Administration Building with David M. Kennedy. I appreciated my relationship with him. On the day I was sustained to the Council of the Twelve Apostles, I walked out of the Salt Lake Tabernacle with Brother Kennedy. I said to him, "David, there must be ten thousand men in this Church more able and qualified to serve in the Council of the Twelve than I am."

Brother Kennedy replied, "No—fifteen thousand."

Brother Kennedy has had a most remarkable career in government, in business, and in the Church. Yet I have found him to be a man of simple faith. He has been Secretary of the Treasury of the United States, U.S. ambassador-at-large, ambassador to the North Atlantic Treaty Organization (NATO), and president and chairman of Continental Illinois Bank. He has also been a missionary, secretary of a mission, a bishop, a member of a stake presidency, and a special ambassador of the First Presidency. He has met with a host of kings, presidents, and heads of state in his lifetime. Yet his faith is basic, pure, and unshakable. He knows where he is going and what is most important in his life. He received this orientation from his father. When young David asked his father, "What are we supposed to be doing here on earth?" his father replied, "We are supposed to be serving God and our fellowman."

To have a simple, untroubled faith, we must accept some absolutes. They are basic. They mean believing that—

1. Jesus, the Son of the Father, is the Christ, the Savior and Redeemer of the world.

2. Joseph Smith was the instrument through which the gospel was restored in its fullness and completeness.

3. The Book of Mormon is the word of God and, as the Prophet Joseph Smith said, the keystone of our religion.

4. Ezra Taft Benson is, as were all of his predecessors as president of the Church, the successor in holding the keys and authority restored by Joseph Smith.

You may ask, "How can I acquire an untroubled faith and a spiritual assurance that each of these absolutes is true?" This untroubled faith can come through prayer, study, and a submissive willingness to keep the commandments. But let us be more specific.

As to the first absolute, accepting Jesus as the Christ, we have two thousand years of teaching and tradition, which help the inquirer accept him as our Savior and Redeemer. So this absolute, initially at least, may be the easiest to accept after study, prayer, and trying to follow his teachings.

The second absolute, the calling of Joseph Smith as the Prophet of the Restoration, may be more difficult for the honest seeker to accept. To have a fair appreciation for the greatness of Joseph Smith's mission, we must step back and view the grand panorama of it all. To me, the only logical explanation for the majesty and success of his work is that he saw what he said he saw, and he was what he said he was. What he restored is so complete, so all-encompassing in concept, so majestic and awesome in potential, that only God himself could have been the author and motivating force behind it. The fruits of Joseph Smith's work, so plain for all to see, are also a testimony of the divinity of his work.

The third absolute, a testimony of the truthfulness of the Book of Mormon, in my opinion comes exactly as Moroni states, by the power of the Holy Ghost after asking God, the Eternal Father, in the name of Christ, if the book is true. The promise then comes: "If ye shall ask with a sincere heart, with real intent, having faith in Christ, he will manifest the truth of it unto you, by the power of the Holy Ghost." (Moroni 10:4.)

The fourth absolute is essential to enjoying an untroubled faith. It is the proposition that President Ezra Taft Benson is the inheritor of the restored keys, as was each of his predecessors since Joseph Smith. Some accept the Savior, the divine mission of Joseph Smith, and the Book of Mormon, but then think that after Joseph's time somehow the Brethren went astray. Many who have thought this have taken others with them, and their efforts have not prospered.

A powerful precedent comes down through the ages to sustain the succession of authority. After the crucifixion of the Savior, Peter, as the senior apostle, became president of the Church. Since the restoration of priesthood keys to Joseph Smith, this practice has been followed in the successions to that office.

As each of the apostles has been ordained to the apostleship and the Quorum of the Twelve, he has been given all of the keys of the kingdom of God on the earth, including some that are to be held inactive until the death of the president of the Church. Upon the death of the president, the keys rest with the Quorum of the Twelve as a body. When a new president is set apart, the Council of the Twelve unitedly lay their hands upon his head and activate the keys he has held since he was ordained an apostle. It has been so since Peter, James, and John bestowed the keys upon the Prophet Joseph Smith. It was so with President Ezra Taft Benson. Because of this transferring of keys and authority, we can truthfully say that since there is priesthood authority on the earth today, President Benson holds the keys to it.

The acceptance of these four absolutes, together with the

ordinances that are administered by the Church and obedience to the commandments, is a solid foundation for the
enjoyment of the promise of the Savior: peace in this life and
eternal life in the life hereafter. (See D&C 59:23.)

I bear my testimony, as one of the special witnesses of
Christ, that the Father and the Son did appear to Joseph Smith
and that he was given direction to reestablish the Church
upon the earth in its fullness. I also testify of the divine and
truthful message of the Book of Mormon. I believe that President Ezra Taft Benson holds all of the keys and authority to
administer the affairs of the kingdom of God on the earth.

Like that man crossing the street in Papeete at four o'clock
in the morning, hurrying to the temple, we can enjoy an
untroubled conscience in the temples of God. Having a
simple, untroubled faith can lift us above the selfish, sordid,
and greedy aspects of the world toward peace and eternal
life.

Chapter 4

FINDING THE ABUNDANT LIFE

The Savior said, "I am come that they might have life, and that they might have it more abundantly." (John 10:10.) How is the abundant life to be obtained? The abundant life involves an endless search for knowledge, light, and truth. President Hugh B. Brown said: "God desires that we learn and continue to learn, but this involves some unlearning. As Uncle Zeke said: 'It ain't my ignorance that done me up but what I know'd that wasn't so.' The ultimate evil is the closing of the mind or steeling it against truth, resulting in the hardening of intellectual arteries." (Baccalaureate Address, Utah State University, June 4, 1965.)

We gain knowledge from two sources. One is the divine and the other is secular. Rex E. Lee has referred to them as "the rational process and the extrarational process." We are all more familiar with the rational process, which we learn in school and through lifelong study. The extrarational or divine source is less common. This source is, however, more sure. Both sources may be available to us. Fortunately, we do not have to choose one to the exclusion of the other. Brother Lee continues, "We should feel equally at home in the academy and in the temple. We should regard each as a center of learning." (*Brigham Young University 1981–82 Fireside and Devotional Speeches*, pp. 131–32.)

We are apparently part of an expanding universe. Secular knowledge is expanding rapidly. Our knowledge of gospel truth is also expanding. Prophets continue to speak. Increased understanding of the scriptures is also possible. And so the opportunities for the abundant life increase as we pursue the quest for truth and knowledge.

In the infinite process of accepting and rejecting information in the search for light, truth, and knowledge, almost everyone may have at one time or another some private questions. That is part of the learning process. Many are like the biblical father of the child with the "dumb spirit" who pleaded with the Savior: "Lord, I believe; help thou mine unbelief." (Mark 9:17, 24.)

The Church has not and, in my opinion, should not speak on every disputed question. But I cannot help wondering if members of the Church do not place themselves in some spiritual peril when publicly disparaging the prophetic calling of Joseph Smith, or his successors, or any of the fundamental, settled doctrines of the Church. Those who express private doubts or unbelief as a public chastisement of the leadership or the doctrine of the Church, or as a confrontation with those also seeking eternal light, have entered upon sacred ground. Those who complain about the doctrines or leadership of the Church but who lack the faith or desire to keep God's commandments risk separating themselves from the divine source of learning. They do not enjoy the same richness of the Spirit that they might enjoy if they proved their sincere love of God by walking humbly before him, by keeping his commandments, and by sustaining those whom he has appointed to lead the Church. Some of those who criticize and find fault have, in the past, felt the peaceful, spiritually settling comfort enjoyed by those in full harmony with the gospel as restored

25

by Joseph Smith. They may also have been lost and forgotten by those who should be more caring.

No stone wall separates the members of the Church from all of the seductions of the world. Members of the Church, like everyone else, are being surfeited with deceptions, challenges, and temptations. However, to those of enduring faith, judgment, and discernment, there is an invisible wall that they choose never to breach. Those on the safe side of this invisible wall are filled with humility, not servitude. They willingly accept the supremacy of God and rely upon the scriptures and counsel of his servants, the leaders of the Church. These leaders are persons with human frailties and are imperfect in their wisdom and judgment. Perfection in individuals is not found on the earth. But almost without exception these leaders sincerely, humbly, and prayerfully render great and dedicated Christian service to the best of their ability. More important, they hold a divine warrant and commission through which great and eternal blessings come to those who sustain and follow them. They are God's servants.

A few may lack understanding of commitment of the faithful. For instance, a critic recently wrote that obedience to commandments such as tithing is mandatory. However, compliance is never mandatory; that is forced. Nothing is mandatory in the Church. Free agency is a cardinal principle of obedience, and obedience comes from love of God and commitment to his work. The only punishment for serious transgression or apostasy is the removal of members from the society and fellowship of the Church. (See D&C 134:10.)

Is personal self-sufficiency one of the reasons men and women may lack faith? Some seem afraid to look to any source of wisdom and knowledge above themselves. They rely only on the secular source of learning. A small number may claim fealty and loyalty to the Church but think it smart, sophisticated, or trendy to be a little rebellious, a little bit independent, and to disparage some of the traditional doctrines handed down by the Prophet Joseph Smith and his successors. This may result from a lack of divine knowledge. When I was a boy, one frequently maligned doctrine was the Word of Wisdom. Some took offense when Church leaders taught it. Now scientific proof, unknown in my youth, has established the Word of Wisdom to be a great law of physical health, even though, in my opinion, its greatest benefits are spiritual.

I have heard some say, "Well, I can believe all of the revelations but one." It is hard to understand this logic. If one believes that revelations come from divine source, how can one pick and choose? Acceptance of the gospel should be complete and absolute, with full heart and soul.

Some want to justify their criticism by claiming, "But it is the truth." My answer is, "How can you be so sure?" Spiritual truth must be bonded to faith and righteousness to be fully understood. The Apostle Paul reminded us that the misuse of the truth changes it into a lie. (See Romans 1:25.)

Since the beginning of the restored Church there has been much opposition, and many critics from both within and without. What have been the results of all this opposition and criticism? Some of the spiritually immature, the weak, and the incredulous have dropped out. The Church itself, however, not only survives, but it grows and strengthens. In some respects nothing in the world is equal to this work. Despite the many challenges of great growth, there are indications of increased faith over much of the earth. For instance, never in the history of the world have so many temples been built.

I do not believe this work will be stopped or seriously

injured by its detractors. There are many prophetic statements to the contrary. History has proven quite conclusively that the Church has grown under persecution; it has prospered under criticism. By finding fault with the doctrines, practices, or leadership, one can waste much time and effort in a fruitless endeavor. Those who have been washed in the waters of baptism put their eternal souls at risk by carelessly pursuing only the secular source of learning. We believe that The Church of Jesus Christ of Latter-day Saints has the fullness of the gospel of Christ, which gospel is the essence of truth and eternal enlightenment. We hold that the great legacy of the Church is that it possesses the only full means for eternal life.

Who is to declare the doctrine? It is well established by revelation and practice that the current president of the Church and his counselors have the keys to declare the doctrine. The investiture of this authority comes from revelation. The First Presidency are constituted "a quorum . . . to receive the oracles for the whole church." (D&C 124:126.) Of this authority, President Stephen L Richards stated:

"They [the Presidency] are the supreme court here on earth in the interpretation of God's law. In the exercise of their functions and delegated powers they are controlled by a constitution, a part of which is written and a part of which is not. The written part consists in authenticated scripture, ancient and modern, and in the recorded utterances of our latter-day prophets. The unwritten part is the spirit of revelation and divine inspiration which are pertinent to their calling. In formulating their interpretations and decisions they always confer with the Council of the Twelve Apostles who by revelation are appointed to assist and act with them in the government of the Church. When, therefore, a judgment is reached and proclaimed by these officers, it becomes binding upon all members of the Church, individual views to the contrary notwithstanding. God's Kingdom is a kingdom of law and order." (Conference Report, October 1938, pp. 115–16.)

We do not wish any who have questions to prove that they are sincere in their feelings by leaving the Church. That is not what we want. We hope that their sincerity would be manifested rather by building upon those feelings that have kept them in the Church. Their faith can be strengthened by following their intuitive judgment and the purest and noblest feelings of their own souls. By looking to a source higher than themselves, they can receive answers to their questions from the divine source. If there have been some mistakes, there is a way back. The doors are wide open; welcoming arms are outstretched. There is a place for all. There is a contribution for each to make.

In the spirit of a letter of Wilford Woodruff to Lyman Wight, an apostle who became separated from the leadership of the Church, we say to all: "Come home to Zion, mingle in our midst, confess and forsake your sins, and do right, as . . . all men have to do, in order to enjoy the favor of God, and the gift of the Holy Ghost, and have fellowship with the Saints. . . . We all feel interested in your welfare; you have no enemies here; the longer you stay away from us, the more alienated your feelings become." (Quoted in Ronald G. Watt, *Brigham Young University Studies,* Autumn 1976, p. 113.)

The leadership of the Church will continue to pray for its critics, its enemies, and those who seek to do it harm.

I believe that few things in life deserve one's complete confidence. I testify that the Church is worthy of full trust. There is no inconsistency between truth and faith. I know that everyone who sincerely and righteously seeks to know this can have it spiritually confirmed. May we open up our minds, hearts, and spirits to the divine source of truth. May we reach above ourselves and beyond our mundane concerns and become heirs to the knowledge of all truth and to the Lord and Savior, Jesus Christ.

Chapter 5

SIX KEYS TO
HEALTHY SELF-ESTEEM

One of the greatest needs of every human being is the
need for positive self-esteem. By this I mean what
we think of ourselves, how we relate to what others think of
us, and how we perceive the value of our accomplishments.

Some mistakenly confuse self-esteem with vanity.
Thomas Carlyle, the famous Scottish author, referred to it as
"the sixth insatiable sense." And Robert Browning, the English poet, said that self-esteem is "an itch for the praise of
fools."

The self-esteem to which I refer is something different. It
is not blind, arrogant, vain love of self, but is self-respecting,
unconceited, honest esteem of ourselves. It is born of inner
peace and strength.

One day I went to get my driver's license renewed. As I
stood in the lines, it was appalling to see the lack of self-
esteem in so many who came to this public office. In the name
of comfort and informality, many were immodestly dressed
and others unkempt. I wondered why they would present
themselves in public so poorly. In their manner of speech
and their dress, they had greatly shortchanged themselves.

Self-esteem goes to the very heart of our personal growth
and accomplishment. Self-esteem is the glue that holds to-

gether our self-reliance, our self-control, our self-approval or disapproval, and keeps all self-defense mechanisms secure. It is a protection against excessive self-deception, self-distrust, self-reproach, and plain, old-fashioned selfishness.

After a lifetime of observing, I have found the greatest respect is owed not necessarily to the rich or the famous, but to the quiet, unsung, unknown heroes whose true identity, like the unknown soldier, is known only to God. The unsung often have little of status, but much of worth.

When I was growing up in the Cottonwood area of Salt Lake County, it was a rural area. One of the men in that area who had great dignity and commanded great respect was an old Scandinavian brother who, after walking a couple of miles, traveled by streetcar to work at the Salt Lake City Cemetery every day. His work was to water and mow the grass, tend the flowers, and dig the graves. He said little because he did not speak English well, but he was always where he should be, doing what he should do in a most dignified, exemplary way. He had no problems with ego or with faith, for while he dug graves for a living, his work was to serve God. He was a man of little status but of great worth.

Not far away from our area was an area where some of the more affluent people of our community lived. Many of them were fine, honorable individuals, but some of them who had much status lived lives of debauchery and drunkenness and little worth.

When the Savior called his disciples, he was not looking for men and women of status, property, or fame. He was looking for those of worth and potential. Those early disciples were an interesting group—some fishermen, a tax gatherer, and others. On one occasion, after some of the apostles were beaten, they went "rejoicing that they were counted worthy to suffer shame for his name." (Acts 5:41.)

Worth has little to do with age. It has everything to do with service. The Lord has made it clear that worthiness is built upon service, not just to family and friends, but also to strangers and even enemies. The great prophet Isaiah gave an eternal warning when he said: "Peace, peace to him that is far off, and to him that is near, saith the Lord; and I will heal him. But the wicked are like the troubled sea, when it cannot rest, whose waters cast up mire and dirt. There is no peace, saith my God, to the wicked." (Isaiah 57:19–21.)

From Milton's *Paradise Lost* comes this truth: "Ofttimes nothing profits more than self-esteem grounded on just and right well managed."

May I suggest six essential keys to keep our self-esteem healthy:

1. *The first key is to keep our free agency.* To keep our free agency, we must not surrender self-control or yield to habits that bind, to addiction that enslaves, or to conduct that destroys. To keep our free agency, we must avoid the deadly traps and pitfalls from which there may be no escape. Some, having been ensnared, spend the best years of their lives trying to escape and so exhaust themselves in the process that in the end they find themselves freed from the addiction but spent, burned out, with their nerves shot and brains forever dulled.

In Proverbs we read: "He that hath no rule over his own spirit is like a city that is broken down, and without walls." (Proverbs 25:28.) To completely enjoy our free agency, it is necessary to follow the counsel of Psalm 119, verse 101: "I have refrained my feet from every evil way." As parents, we should follow the counsel of Alma and teach our children to "withstand every temptation of the devil" (Alma 37:33) and to "bridle all [their] passions" (Alma 38:12).

2. *The second key to adequate self-esteem is humility.* By hu-

mility I do not refer to "breast beating" or "sackcloth and ashes." I refer to the humility that comes with inner strength and peace. This is the humility that helps us to accept and live with our own warts without cosmetics to hide them. It is important to learn to live with our incorrectable physical and mental defects without comment and without explanation.

A few years ago I became acquainted with a delightful new friend. He is charming, outgoing, and well groomed. He is a successful businessman. His spirituality shines through his countenance. He was completely honest in our business relationship. After many contacts and several months I noticed that he walked with a slight limp, which had not been obvious before. That led to closer observation. It was surprising that when I looked past the gracious smile, I noticed that my friend was slightly hunchbacked, with a somewhat misshapen spine. These physical defects were so well hidden by natural goodness, warmth, and great charm that they were as nothing in the total man. My friend accepts his physical defects with humility and strength and completely compensates for them with his natural personality.

There is another dimension of humility that must be mentioned, that of being teachable. The prophet Samuel counseled, "Now therefore stand still, that I may reason with you." (1 Samuel 12:7.) Proverbs reminds us that "whoso loveth instruction loveth knowledge." (Proverbs 12:1.) Any married man should be humble enough to learn from his wife. When Sara Merrill married N. Eldon Tanner, he was a schoolteacher from a farm in Alberta, Canada. Instead of bridling at receiving suggestions from his wife, President Tanner had the humility and the strength to listen.

3. *The third key to self-esteem is honesty.* Honesty begins with being true to one's own self.

Some years ago I sat as a spectator in a courtroom drama concerning the custody of some children. The contention was that the natural mother was not a good housekeeper, which was intended to add fuel to the claim that she was an unfit mother. A caseworker testified that when she visited the family home, it was in shambles and the kitchen was dirty.

Then the mother was called to the stand. A middle-aged, heavy, physically unattractive lady came forward, took the oath, and sat in the witness stand. The attorney for the father, who had remarried and wanted custody of the children, followed up relentlessly on the testimony already provided by the caseworker. His questions to the beleaguered mother were penetrating.

"Isn't it a fact," he asked, "that your house was as dirty as a pigpen the day the caseworker came?"

What drama! How could the mother answer in her own best interest and protect her custody of the children? What should she say? There was electricity in the air. She hesitated for a tense moment, and then she responded, calmly, with complete self-assurance: "Yes, my house certainly was a mess that day."

Her honesty obviously surprised even the judge, who leaned over the bench and asked, "What do you mean, 'that day'?"

"Well, your honor," she replied, "earlier that morning I had been bottling peaches. I had peeled, cooked, and bottled two bushels of peaches. I had not finished cleaning up the mess when the caseworker came. My sink was still sticky from the syrup that had spilled over when I poured it into the bottles before they sealed. My house certainly was a mess that day. I try to be a good housekeeper, but with three children I can't possibly keep it straight all the time."

Her frankness and candor were absolutely disarming, and

35

devastating to the opposition. When she finished, everyone in the courtroom knew the judge would rule in her favor. As she arose and stepped down from the witness stand, she had the bearing and the self-assurance of a queen. Being true to one's own self is the essence of honesty, and a keystone of self-esteem.

4. *The fourth key to self-esteem is the love of work.* The most gifted athlete at our university excelled at every sport. He played football and ran the hurdles—in fact, he held the conference record in the low hurdles. Our coach, Ike Armstrong, required that the sprinters run once a week with the quarter milers for 300 yards to increase the stamina of the sprinters and increase the speed of the quarter milers. My friend would lead all of the runners for about 275 yards, but as soon as the first quarter miler passed him he would quit and wouldn't even finish. His natural talent and ability were such that he never had to extend himself to excel. He married, but the marriage failed. He went on to play professional football and was something of a star until he started taking drugs. He died from the debilitating effects of drugs and alcohol. Others with much less talent have achieved far more.

In my observation, there are very few people who are of true genius. Many are gifted, but most of the world's work and great accomplishments come from ordinary people with talent that they develop. An ordinary talent can be nurtured and nourished into a great gift through hard work. Some of the artisans of China spend years making one exquisite art object of unbelievable grace and beauty.

Some time ago we went to hear the New York Philharmonic in concert in Salt Lake City. The music was exceptional, the teamwork of the gifted musicians blending to make a superb orchestral sound. Each member of the group possesses great talent. Not everyone, however, has a talent for the arts.

Some may have a gift to make others feel important, happy, and special. This gift should also be developed and strengthened.

The spiritual gifts likewise can be refined and enlarged by attentive application to righteous living, to prayer, to study of the scriptures, and to obedience. Film producer George Lucas has said, "It doesn't matter what people say about me or what I say. What matters is what I accomplish." What we accomplish helps our self-esteem. Frequently we hear, "The work I do is unimportant," or "I'm just this or that." Every job that has to be done is important; no matter how minimal it seems, someone has to do it.

During major floods in Utah a few summers ago, a million sandbags had to be filled, tied, and put into place. The former head of one of the biggest companies in Utah wanted to be helpful in his neighborhood. The bishop who was directing some of the work in that area asked this man to find tie strings and to tie sandbags. He found tie strings in many places, including some on the ground, and he went around picking up the strings. It was an emergency. Someone had to do it.

5. *The fifth key to building self-esteem is the ability to love.* The Savior commanded us to love others and ourselves. Are we secure enough in our love of ourselves to laugh at ourselves, to admit mistakes, to graciously accept compliments? Are we secure enough in our love of others to smile and say hello to strangers? Years ago in seminary our class was taught:

> I have to live with myself, and so
> I want to be fit for myself to know.
> I want to go out with my head erect;
> I want to demand all men's respect.
> I never can hide myself from me;
> I see what others may never see.

I can never fool myself, and so,
Whatever happens, I want to be
Self-respecting and conscience-free.

6. *The sixth and most essential key to self-esteem is love of God.*
Mosiah asked, "How knoweth the man the master whom he
has not served?" (Mosiah 5:13.) In his epistle to Titus, Paul
said that many "profess that they know God; but in works
they deny him." (Titus 1:16.)

A key is given to us: "Hereby we know that he abideth
in us, by the Spirit which he hath given us." (1 John 3:24.)
We can know that we know God "if we keep his commandments. He that saith, I know him, and keepeth not his commandments, is a liar, and the truth is not in him." (1 John
2:3–4.)

The self-esteem of many has been devastated by the loss
of loved ones, by divorce, by other personal misfortunes.
Some carry an extra burden of guilt from grievous sins.
Transgression is devastating to self-esteem, and after transgression usually comes rationalization, and often lying. This
is what makes justice so violent to the offending.

Fortunately we have the great principle of repentance
whereby sins "as scarlet" can become "white as snow." (Isaiah 1:18.) I am grateful for this principle and pray that no one
will hesitate to find the peace that comes from repentance.
It is important to remember and never forget that all of us,
male and female, were created in the image of God and created
by God. Mankind is the noblest of all creations.

"What is man," asked the Psalmist, "that thou art mindful
of him? and the son of man, that thou visitest him? For thou
hast made him a little lower than the angels, and hast crowned
him with glory and honour. Thou madest him to have dominion over the works of thy hands; thou hast put all things
under his feet." (Psalm 8:4–6.)

Frequently in my ministry, as I have been setting apart an individual to a calling in the Church, the distinct impression has come to me that the person on whose head I have laid hands was foreordained to that calling. To the prophet Jeremiah came this assurance from the Lord: "Before I formed thee in the belly I knew thee; and before thou camest forth out of the womb I sanctified thee, and I ordained thee a prophet unto the nations." (Jeremiah 1:5.)

Not all of us are called to leadership in the kingdom. Yet, is there a greater work than that of teacher, father, or mother? So it is that nobody is nobody. The seeds of divinity are in all of us. There will come a day when we will have to account to God for what we have done with that portion of divinity which is within us.

I testify that God loves each of us, warts and all. I testify that he knows the name of each of us. I testify that each of us has a potential in this life and beyond the grave that exceeds our fondest dreams.

Chapter 6

THE NEED FOR
BALANCE IN OUR LIVES

M any people today are concerned only with single interests, judging the merits of candidates and causes on the basis of those single issues. In the Church, some have been concerned with one principle or one phase of the gospel over all others.

The wise Job said, "Let me be weighed in an even balance, that God may know my integrity." (Job 31:6.) As we employ an even balance, so also we shall be judged, for the measure by which we judge comes back to judge us. The Savior taught, "Judge not, that ye be not judged. For with what judgment ye judge, ye shall be judged: and with what measure ye mete, it shall be measured to you again." (Matthew 7:1–2.)

In recent years there seem to have been many whose lives have been spent protesting. Perhaps they have felt to do this because they have felt repressed, or wished to bring about change, or have acted out of selfish reasons, thinking that if they tore the house down they might end up with a shingle. Some protestors have said that they have done so in order to be free—free of traditions, free of morals, free of all of the confining standards of society, unrestrained by government or law. Some have been wildly self-indulgent. As Harry Emerson Fosdick noted, they have "habits that bind them, diseases that curse them, and blasted reputations that ruin them."

Those who have succumbed to this kind of personal disaster often find that the balance in their lives becomes somewhat tilted and uneven. Many people expend far too much precious energy in protesting the rules. Since they did not make the rules, some feel that they should not be restricted by them. Others make a game of testing the fences to see what they can get away with. Some think that by breaking the rules they somehow become stronger or independent. Those who fight the rules spend much time and energy trying to express independence in their quest to find identity. And having traveled far down this road, they find that this is not the road to freedom, but to slavery.

Talents, gifts of expression, and precious time are exhausted in swimming against too many tides. I have no hesitancy in suggesting that young men can learn to express themselves better through excellence in the classroom or on the playing field than in the length of their hair. Young women can obtain a better identity and receive better notice through academic excellence and artistic expression than through immodesty of dress.

There are times when each of us has to have some gumption to take a stand as to what we wish to preserve or change in order to maintain our self-respect and not be as "a reed shaken with the wind." (Matthew 11:7.) We need to take our great stands in life on moral issues, not kicking against the rules of dress or behavior in society, appearing to be eccentric or unbalanced or immature. We lose much credibility and strength, and risk being weighed on an uneven balance, when, Don Quixote–like, we go around "tilting windmills."

For each of us, a transcendent blessing is available when we make the right moral choices. It is much easier for those who have a righteous balance to yield to "the enticings of the Holy Spirit." (Mosiah 3:19.) Then we can leave behind the attributes of the natural man or woman and become someone much more enlightened. Alma counseled his brethren to "contend no more against the Holy Ghost." (Alma 34:38.) The gifts of the Holy Ghost have special strengths for those who study and learn. "He shall teach you all things, and bring all things to your remembrance." (John 14:26.) Yes, "the Holy Ghost shall be thy constant companion, and . . . it shall flow unto thee forever and ever." (D&C 121:46.)

How do these marvelous gifts function? Parley P. Pratt stated: "It quickens all the intellectual faculties; increases, enlarges, expands and purifies all the natural passions and affections. It adopts them by the gift of wisdom to their lawful use. It inspires virtue, kindness, goodness, tenderness, gentleness and charity. It develops beauty of person, form and features. It invigorates all the faculties of the physical and intellectual man. It strengthens and gives tone to the nerves. In short, it is as it were marrow to the bone, joy to the heart, light to the eyes, music to the ears, and life to the whole being." Persons enjoying these gifts have "light of their countenance," and their presence is "a warm glow of pure gladness and sympathy of spirit." (*Key to the Science of Theology,* 1891, pp. 101–3.)

An important part of the gospel message is that we not be too rigid: that we open up our minds, develop some tolerance, and not be quick to render judgment. I learned when I was making my living in the arena that we do not always have all of the facts. There always seemed to be at least two sides to a question. Everything is not just black and white. The counsel of the Savior as he instructed his Twelve was, "Behold, I send you forth as sheep in the midst of wolves; be ye therefore wise as serpents, and harmless as doves." (Matthew 10:16.)

It is not always easy to achieve appropriate balance. In

addition to what we read in the newspapers, we can have brought right into our homes in color most of the problems of an entire world. We also have our own personal ups and downs and challenges. The stresses of life are real and rather constant. There is, however, a defense against much of this. A thoughtful man said, "There is no defense against adverse fortune which is, on the whole, so effectual as an habitual sense of wonder." (Thomas Wentworth Storrow Higginson.) Humor is a defense against adversity.

For many years as I have blessed newborn children, including my own, I have blessed them with a sense of humor. I do this with the hope that it will help guard them against being too rigid, that they will have balance in their lives, and that situations and problems and difficulties will not be overdrawn.

Many years ago in one of the courtrooms of Utah, a divorce case was called for a hearing. One of the participating attorneys, indignant and incensed, took the witness stand to bring before the court the fact that just the night before, the husband and the wife had reconciled their differences. He urged that because of the reconciliation, his adversary was unprincipled, unfair, and unethical in now coming into court.

The judge turned to the other attorney and asked him if he were going to take the witness stand to refute the allegations against his character. The defamed attorney, a wise and experienced counselor, said, "Oh, no, your honor. I'm not going to take the witness stand. He might be able to prove all those allegations against me." The courtroom broke into laughter, the tension was broken, and things quickly got put into proper place.

Thomas Carlyle stated, "True humor springs not more from the head than from the heart. It is not contempt. Its essence is love. Its issue is not in laughter, but in still smiles

43

which lie far deeper." And Abraham Lincoln said, "With the fearful strain that is on me night and day, if I did not live I should die."

Cultivating good humor may be helpful in finding our own identity. Young people who are trying to find out who they really are often have concerns as to their ability to meet and cope with the challenges that confront them and that lie ahead. They will find that it is easier to ride over the bumps and come quickly to their own identity if they cultivate the good humor that comes naturally. It is important that we all learn to laugh at ourselves and poke fun at ourselves.

An important dimension in learning to laugh at ourselves lies in not being afraid to make a mistake. When I was a bishop, we sought to have a ward choir. We had a good leader, Brother Anderson. However, he encouraged the bishop to sing in the choir. I felt that as a measure of support for Brother Anderson and the others, I should try to sing with them—but things went from bad to worse.

Brother Anderson liked to invite the choir members to improve their talents by singing solos. One Sunday during choir practice he asked that the bishop sing a small solo. I found it very difficult to turn him down in front of the choir, so during sacrament meeting, when the choir sang I tried to sing the solo. I was so frightened that the paper trembled in my hand, and I could hardly hold it. I felt embarrassed and humiliated. All of my mask of dignity was gone.

After the meeting, as I walked down the aisle, I was met with warm smiles and expressions of understanding and support. Someone said, "Bishop, it surely makes us feel good to see you scared." That day the bishop became more human.

Our leaders have demonstrated that one can enjoy both faith and humor. It was said of President Heber C. Kimball that he prayed and conversed with God "as one man talketh to another." However, "on one occasion while offering an earnest appeal on behalf of certain of his fellow creatures he startled the kneeling circle by bursting into a loud laugh in the midst of his prayer. Quickly regaining his composure and solemn address, he remarked apologetically, 'Lord, it makes me laugh to pray about some people.' " (*Life of Heber C. Kimball*, Salt Lake City: Bookcraft, 1967, p. 427.) This sense of humor was not lost on his grandson, President Spencer W. Kimball.

Another man who had a great sense of humor and enthusiasm was Elder LeGrand Richards. One day a stake president came to my office to see me. On the way out, he stopped to see Elder Richards, who would be coming to his stake in a week or two. He asked, "Brother Richards, how are you?" That great apostle said, "Well, president, I will tell you. My body, the house I live in, is getting old and creaky." Then he added, with all ninety-five years of his life testifying, "But the real LeGrand Richards is on fire."

A good sense of humor will help us hone our talents. One of the talents that needs to be greatly magnified is sensitivity to others, and this involves reaching out and touching another heart. By learning not to be afraid of ourselves, we are able to stir up kindred feelings for others. Under the cultivation of the Holy Ghost, our talents become greatly magnified.

Balance in large measure is knowing the things that can be changed and put in proper perspective and recognizing the things that will not change. Much of the rest in obtaining sound balance lies in attitude. May our attitude be one of achieving balance and wisdom and understanding in all that we do.

Chapter 7

DOING THE BEST THINGS
IN THE WORST OF TIMES

In Leicester, England, an inscription on the outside wall of an old church reads, "In the year 1654 when all things were, throughout this nation, either demolished or profaned, Sir Robert Shirley, Baronet, founded and built this church. He it is whose singular praise it is to have done the best things in the worst times, and to have hoped them in the most calamitous."

We have recently been in unsettling times economically. Interest rates have risen so high that many cannot obtain a home. People are unable to borrow money without having the interest eat up business profits and wages. Income tax laws seem to encourage borrowing but not saving. For many of us, the times are always difficult. For others, the times are particularly difficult when we are struggling to qualify and to prepare ourselves for our life's career and activities. In the face of such difficulties, well might we ask, What are the best things we can do in the worst times?

World War II was a difficult time for many of us. My beloved Ruth and I were married early in the war years. We loved each other and wanted to be together as much as possible before I went overseas. During my training we crossed the United States ten times and went to Canada and Mexico.

All of this travel was a severe strain on our meager army income. We had both been taught to pay our tithing; we believed in the law, and we kept the law. All my life I have enjoyed paying tithing. It has made me feel good to pay it, and I feel more secure when it is paid. But one month when we had a transfer across the United States, it took all of our money to get from one part of the country to the other. That month we postponed the paying of our tithing. In all my life I have not had such serious financial strain as we had when we were behind on our tithing.

In order to augment my meager army pay, Ruth, having no children at the time, went to work while we concentrated on getting our tithing caught up. We felt that in those difficult days, paying our tithing was the best thing for us to do, and it proved to be right. During all the rest of our married years we have paid our tithing as the income came in, willingly and happily.

One of the greatest lessons I have learned during my lifetime about doing the best things in the worst times is that people who pay their tithing in both difficult times and good times get along better. They simply have fewer problems; there are fewer family problems and fewer financial problems. Their outlook is more positive, their ability to do and function is increased, and they prosper spiritually as well as temporally.

The principle of tithing was given and its blessings proved thousands of years ago. In the Old Testament we read:

"And as soon as the commandment came abroad, the children of Israel brought in abundance the firstfruits of corn, wine, and oil, and honey, and of all the increase of the field; and the tithe of all things brought they abundantly. And concerning the children of Israel and Judah, that dwelt in the cities of Judah, they also brought in the tithe of oxen and sheep, and the tithe of holy things which were consecrated unto the Lord their God, and laid them by heaps. . . .

"Then Hezekiah questioned with the priests and the Levites concerning the heaps. And Azariah the chief priest of the house of Zadok answered him, and said, Since the people began to bring the offerings into the house of the Lord, we have had enough to eat, and have left plenty: for the Lord hath blessed his people; and that which is left is this great store." (2 Chronicles 31:5–6, 9–10.)

When I grew up in the Cottonwood area of the Salt Lake Valley, President Henry D. Moyle was our stake president. Years passed and I became bishop of our ward. President Moyle, in the intervening years, was called to the Council of the Twelve and later to the First Presidency. Like the other faithful members of the ward, President Moyle always came to tithing settlement. Invariably each year he would make out a check for the balance of his tithing. As he handed me the check, he always said, "Bishop, this is a full tithe and a little bit more because that's the way we have been blessed."

I am grateful for the faithfulness of the Saints in keeping the law of the tithe. I believe that no other people on the face of the earth are as faithful in keeping this great law as are our Latter-day Saints.

Recently I was with a bishop of another faith in a distant city. His congregation meets in one of the greatest cathedrals in the country, a national shrine, a building of superb architecture and construction. I said to him, "Bishop, it must take a great deal of money to operate this cathedral."

The smile left his face, and he said, "Yes, we still owe many millions of dollars on it, much of which is interest-bearing. I don't have time to pursue my ministry the way I would like because I have to raise funds to pay off the debt of the cathedral."

Without trying to be offensive, I said, "Bishop, there is an answer to the money concerns of your congregation and the cathedral."

He looked interested. I mentioned the law of tithing.

The bishop said, "Oh, I believe in tithing, but our people have not yet learned to tithe."

Again, being a little bit bold, but hopefully not offensive, I said, "But the law of the tithe has to be taught when we are children." He agreed and said he would have to work on teaching tithing.

Knowing something of the faithfulness of many of our people in this regard, I rejoiced in being a member of a tithe-paying people.

Sister Antonietta Oliveira, a worker in the Sao Paulo Temple, believed in and paid tithing for fifty years before she joined the Church. It was a schooling for her and her family preparatory to baptism. Her son Saul has served as a bishop, stake president, mission president, and regional representative. Her grandsons have served on missions.

I have come to believe that while tithing is a money law, it is more a law of faith and obedience. President Spencer W. Kimball said: "In faith we plant the seed, and soon we see the miracle of the blossoming. Men have often misunderstood and have reversed the process. They would have the harvest before the planting, the reward before the service, the miracle before the faith. Even the most demanding labor unions would hardly ask the wages before the labor. But many of us would have the vigor without the observance of the health laws, prosperity through the opened windows of heaven without the payment of our tithes. We would have the close communion with our Father without fasting and praying; we would have rain in due season and peace in the land without observing the Sabbath and keeping the other commandments

49

of the Lord. We would pluck the rose before planting the roots; we would harvest the grain before its planting and cultivating." (Conference Report, October 1952, p. 47.)

In order to know when to do the best things in the worst times, we can heed the counsel of President Joseph F. Smith, who said, "One of the best ways I know of to pay my obligations to my brother, my neighbor or business associate, is for me first to pay my obligations to the Lord. I can pay more of my debts to my neighbors, if I contracted them, after I have met my honest obligations with the Lord, than I can by neglecting the latter; and you can do the same. If you desire to prosper, and to be free men and women and a free people, first meet your just obligations to God, and then meet your obligations to your fellowmen." (Conference Report, April 1903, p. 2.)

Meeting our obligations to God and then meeting our obligations to others is the best thing to do in all times, good or bad.

I am grateful that the law of tithing, like the other principles of the gospel, is not compulsory. I am grateful to the Lord for his wisdom in making the law simple: one-tenth of our increase. I am grateful that over the years the brethren have not made interpretations of that simple law. The law of tithing is not like the law of the Medes and the Persians, filled with technicalities that would take away the simplicity of it. A little Primary rhyme teaches the simplicity of the law:

> I know what tithing is,
> I'll tell you every time;
> Ten cents from a dollar
> And a penny from a dime.

Tithing is a tenth. Each individual must determine for

himself or herself what a full tithe is. It is between the individual and the Lord.

To do the best things in the worst times, we should also keep the great companion law to tithing, the law of the fast. In keeping this law, we will receive blessings that are unique and different and separate from those associated with the law of tithing. As I understand the twenty-fifth chapter of Matthew, we will be in large measure judged by the manner in which we keep the law of the fast:

"When the Son of man shall come in his glory, and all the holy angels with him, then shall he sit upon the throne of his glory: and before him shall be gathered all nations: and he shall separate them one from another, as a shepherd divideth his sheep from the goats: and he shall set the sheep on his right hand, but the goats on the left.

"Then shall the King say unto them on his right hand, Come, ye blessed of my Father, inherit the kingdom prepared for you from the foundation of the world: for I was an hungred, and ye gave me meat: I was thirsty, and ye gave me drink: I was a stranger, and ye took me in: naked, and ye clothed me: I was sick, and ye visited me: I was in prison, and ye came unto me.

"Then shall the righteous answer him, saying, Lord, when saw we thee an hungred, and fed thee? or thirsty, and gave thee drink? When saw we thee a stranger, and took thee in? or naked, and clothed thee? Or when saw we thee sick, or in prison, and came unto thee?

"And the King shall answer and say unto them, Verily I say unto you, Inasmuch as ye have done it unto one of the least of these my brethren, ye have done it unto me."

The King also has some harsh words to say to those who do not give of their substance to those who are hungry and have no meat or who are thirsty or naked or sick or in prison:

51

"Verily I say unto you, Inasmuch as ye did it not to one of the least of these, ye did it not to me. And these shall go away into everlasting punishment: but the righteous into life eternal." (Matthew 25:31–40, 45–46.)

Keeping the law of the fast allows us to begin to fulfill our obligations to those in need.

In recent times of high inflation, a philosophy has developed that we should buy now and pay later. I cannot believe that this is sound practice for the Latter-day Saints. There always comes a day of reckoning. Many people who have not managed their debts will find themselves in difficulty. Over the years the wise counsel of our leaders has been to avoid debt except for the purchase of a home or to pay for an education. I have not heard any of the prophets change this counsel. In times of severe inflation there is other wise counsel to be followed. We can obtain and lay aside our year's supply of food, commodities, clothing, and, where possible, fuel.

Occasionally someone in the Church is considered for a calling who is not ready to accept it. An interview reveals that the person under consideration does not have his or her personal affairs in order. There is a large debt to be serviced, or the standard of living the family has become accustomed to requires great expenditures of money and there are no resources available to fall back on. One of the best things we can do in the worst of times is to plan and work to arrange our affairs so that we can be available to accept the calls that might come to us from the Lord.

Maintaining integrity in all financial dealings is another necessary ingredient during all times, good or bad. Many years ago a friend of mine bought some furniture on an installment plan that was financed by the owner of the furniture store. Shortly thereafter my friend lost his job and was faced with making the furniture payments with only four dollars in his pocket to feed and clothe his family. Instead of ignoring the proprietor of the store and permitting the account to go delinquent, my friend went to him and said, "I have lost my job and can't make the installment payment on the furniture. I have four dollars to feed and clothe my family. I will give you the four dollars as the installment or, if you wish, I will bring the furniture back."

The proprietor told my friend that he appreciated his integrity in coming in and telling him of his problem, and that he should keep the four dollars; the store would carry him until he got a job and could resume the payments. In time, employment was obtained and the debt was paid off. Over the ensuing years my friend bought other furniture from the same store, and because of his integrity the proprietor considered him a valuable customer.

In our society we value the successes and achievements of others, and we admire those who are able to start and manage profitable businesses or become successful professionally. Successes should be obtained, however, through integrity in all transactions. Success has a price, and the price has to be paid. Successful operations based upon something for nothing do not exist.

Installment buying on easy terms has trapped many well-intentioned people into positions they did not foresee or intend. Credit cards, charge cards, and consumer credit devices must be used sparingly and wisely. Full payment with cash upon purchase is still sound policy in good times or bad, because installments carry high interest.

An equally important guideline in the management of personal affairs is to live within our income and have some means to spare for emergencies and for future needs.

The love of money is the root of many evils because it

often involves selfishness. On the other hand, the wise use of money involves principles of righteousness. It involves sacrifice and discipline. It is the acid test of our faith. Many of the Savior's parables made reference to money in one form or another.

Yes, these are hard times. But when we meet our obligations first to God and then to others, we will find success and happiness.

Chapter 8

INTEGRITY, THE MOTHER
OF MANY VIRTUES

Integrity is defined in the dictionary as firm adherence to a code of moral values. It connotes soundness and incorruptibility. It is the mother of many virtues. It begins when we deal justly with ourselves.

Walter Spat, the first stake president in South America, for many years has owned a furniture factory in Sao Paulo, Brazil. The delicately handcarved roses, figures, and designs in the beautiful woods make his furniture as lovely as any I have ever seen. Every piece is exquisite. Every creation is a masterpiece. One day my wife, Ruth, and I were in his factory when a beautiful, newly made piece of furniture was brought in for showing. The grain of the wood flowed beautifully, and the finish was perfect. But to President Spat, the hardware did not seem up to standard. Without hesitation, he took a screwdriver and a pair of pliers and pulled off all the hardware, commenting, "That is not my work." President Spat seems incapable of making a piece of furniture that is not as perfect as it can be. His work reflects his honor and integrity.

Ralph Waldo Emerson stated: "Every man takes care that his neighbor shall not cheat him. But a day comes when he begins to care that he do[es] not cheat his neighbor. Then all goes well. He has changed his market-cart into a chariot of the sun." (From *Conduct of Life*.)

Integrity is the value we set on ourselves. It is a fulfillment of the duty we owe ourselves. Honorable individuals will personally commit to live up to certain self-imposed expectations. They need no outside check or control. They are honorable in their inner core.

Where best does the soul play its part? Is it in outward show? Or is it within, where no mortal eyes can penetrate and where we have an inner defense against the tragedies of life?

Integrity is the light that shines from a disciplined conscience. It is the strength of duty within us. Moses gave the following counsel: "If a man vow a vow unto the Lord, or swear an oath to bind his soul with a bond; he shall not break his word, he shall do according to all that proceedeth out of his mouth." (Numbers 30:2.)

The power of keeping an oath was manifested by Nephi, who held Zoram, the frightened servant of Laban, to keep him from fleeing. Dr. Hugh Nibley has written:

"Nephi, a powerful fellow, held the terrified Zoram in a vise-like grip long enough to swear a solemn oath in his ear, 'as the Lord liveth, and as I live' (1 Nephi 4:32), that he would not harm him if he would listen. Zoram immediately relaxed, and Nephi swore another oath to him that he would be a free man if he would join the party. . . . As soon as Zoram 'made an oath unto us that he would tarry with us from that time forth . . . our fears did cease concerning him.' (1 Nephi 4:35, 37.)" (*An Approach to the Book of Mormon,* Salt Lake City: Deseret Book, 1976, pp. 103–4.)

At times being true to oneself requires extraordinary strength and courage. For instance, in the early days of the Church it was very unpopular, even dangerous, to uphold Joseph Smith as a prophet of God. Lyman Wight was one of those imprisoned by the leaders of a mob in 1839. General

Wilson advised Brother Wight, "We do not wish to hurt you nor kill you," and then, following an oath, said, "but we have one thing against you, and that is, you are too friendly to Joe Smith. . . . Wight, you know all about his character."

Brother Wight said, "I do, sir."

"Will you swear all you know concerning him?" asked General Wilson.

Brother Wight told General Wilson he "believed . . . Joseph Smith to be the most philanthropic man he ever saw, and possessed of the most pure . . . principles—a friend to mankind, a maker of peace."

General Wilson then observed, "Wight, I fear your life is in danger, for there is no end to the prejudice against Joe Smith."

"Kill and be damned, sir," was Brother Wight's answer.

Returning later that night, General Wilson told Lyman Wight: "I regret to tell you your die is cast; your doom is fixed; you are sentenced to be shot tomorrow morning on the public square in Far West, at eight o'clock."

Brother Wight answered, "Shoot, and be damned."

The decree of execution of the prisoners was revoked the next morning. (*History of the Church* 3:446–47.)

Dealing justly with oneself lays a foundation for dealing justly with others. During World War II, I came home on leave early one September. It was time to put peaches in bottles to preserve them for winter. My beloved mother-in-law called an old friend, George B. Andrus. The conversation on the telephone was brief:

"George, do you have any peaches for sale?"

"I have a few, but they are not very good."

I volunteered to drive Mother Wright to pick up the peaches. When we arrived she said, "George, where are your peaches?"

Brother Andrus opened his garage door, and I saw bushel baskets filled with large, golden fruit with red kisses from sun ripening. Each basket was filled so full that when I lifted one into the trunk of the car, some of the luscious peaches on top rolled off and bruised. Brother Andrus immediately replaced them with other perfect ones.

On the way home I said to Mother Wright, "What did he mean when he said his fruit was not very good?"

She answered, "If you knew George Andrus, you would know that any fruit he would put on the market would be good and that he would give more than full value."

I wondered what the fruit would have been like if George had said it was good. Brother Andrus's self-imposed expectations led him to go beyond what we expected of him in his dealings with us.

Natural, inherent integrity is manifested almost every hour of every day of our lives. Those who unjustly profit at the expense of others may gain a fortune, but they forfeit something more important—their own integrity. Taking advantage of others is a counterfeit form of true success and honor.

Those who have children and are involved in doing something less than they should be doing may be involved in a double evil, for in addition to the inherent wrong they commit, they also teach another generation to do wrong. There seems to be an immutable law that children may take license from what their parents do and expand upon it, confirming the old adage that the chickens not only come home to roost, but they bring their chicks with them.

Performance of duty, regardless of the sacrifice involved, is a part of dealing justly with oneself and others. Early in the history of the Salt Lake Valley, Joseph W. McMurrin was placed in charge of guarding some of the leaders of the

Church. Once a meeting was held in Social Hall in Salt Lake City and an intruder under a claim of authority tried to enter. Joseph W. McMurrin, being true to his trust to guard the servants of the Lord, restrained the man from entering. President Heber J. Grant related that the intruder "finally got his hand loose and took his pistol and, pressing it against Brother McMurrin's body, fired two bullets. . . . Those bullets lodged just under the skin in his back. He was attended by Dr. Joseph Benedict who told Joseph W. McMurrin that no man could live after two bullets had passed through his vitals, and then added: 'If you wish to make a dying statement you should do so immediately.'

"I went with John Henry Smith to brother McMurrin's home and saw where the flesh was burned away around those terrible gaping wounds. I saw where the bullets had gone clear through him. I heard John Henry Smith say, 'By the authority of the Priesthood of the living God which we hold, and in the name of the Lord, Jesus Christ, we say that you shall be made absolutely whole, and that there shall be no physical weakness left upon your body because of these terrible wounds that you have received while guarding the servants of the living God.' " President Grant concluded this talk, which he gave on November 21, 1931: "Joseph W. McMurrin is alive and well, and has never had any physical weakness because of those terrible wounds." (*Gospel Standards,* Salt Lake City: Improvement Era, 1969, pp. 310–11.)

It is difficult to be just with oneself and others unless we recognize the law of the harvest. We reap what we sow. Latter-day Saints have long been taught to live by the virtues of independence, industry, thrift, and self-reliance. Working for what we receive is a cardinal, timeless principle of self-respect. The whole world admires success. But how each of us defines success and how we seek it is crucial to our happiness.

The fruits of industry and thrift may appropriately be put into sound investments. A good, solid investment can equal years of toil, and there is some risk in all that we do. But investments that are highly speculative and promoted with unsound, vague promises of inordinate return should be viewed carefully. The leaders of the Church have long warned against speculation. Brigham Young said, "If the Lord ever revealed anything to me, he has shown me that the Elders of Israel must let speculation alone and attend to the duties of their calling." (*Journal of Discourses* 8:179.)

In our time President Nathan Eldon Tanner said: "Investment debt should be fully secured so as not to encumber a family's security. Don't invest in speculative ventures. The spirit of speculation can become intoxicating. Many fortunes have been wiped out by the uncontrolled appetite to accumulate more and more. Let us learn from the sorrows of the past and avoid enslaving our time, energy, and general health to a gluttonous appetite to acquire increased material goods." (Conference Report, October 1979, p. 120.)

What is success? Is it money? Is it achievement? Is it fame? Is it position? Is it dominion? The prophet Micah defined success as follows: "He hath shewed thee, O man, what is good; and what doth the Lord require of thee, but to do justly, and to love mercy, and to walk humbly with thy God?" (Micah 6:8.)

The prophet Ezekiel also gave a formula for success: "But if a man be just, and do that which is lawful and right, . . . and hath not oppressed any, but hath restored to the debtor his pledge, hath spoiled none by violence, hath given his bread to the hungry, and hath covered the naked with a garment, . . . hath walked in my statutes, and hath kept my judgments, to deal truly; he is just, he shall surely live, saith the Lord God." (Ezekiel 18:5, 7, 9.)

The Lord appeared to Solomon in a dream and said, "Ask what I shall give thee." Solomon replied, "Give therefore thy servant an understanding heart to judge thy people, that I may discern between good and bad." (1 Kings 3:5, 9.) The Lord was pleased because Solomon had not asked for success as the world defines it.

Complete and constant integrity is a great law of human conduct. There need to be some absolutes in life. Some things should never be done, some lines should never be crossed, some vows should never be broken, some words should never be spoken, and some thoughts should never be entertained.

Yet there is a place for mercy, for equity, and for forgiveness. Even the stalwart Peter, the chief apostle, was forgiven for a moment of weakness. Luke records what happened when the chief priests and others took Jesus to the high priest's house:

"And Peter followed afar off. And when they had kindled a fire in the midst of the hall, and were set down together, Peter sat down among them. But a certain maid beheld him as he sat by the fire, and earnestly looked upon him, and said, This man was also with him [Jesus]. And he denied him, saying, Woman, I know him not.

"And after a little while another saw him, and said, Thou art also of them. And Peter said, Man, I am not.

"And about the space of one hour after another confidently affirmed, saying, Of a truth this fellow also was with him: for he is a Galilean. And Peter said, Man, I know not what thou sayest.

"And immediately, while he yet spake, the cock crew. And the Lord turned, and looked upon Peter. And Peter remembered the word of the Lord, how he had said unto him, Before the cock crow, thou shalt deny me thrice.

"And Peter went out, and wept bitterly." (Luke 22:54–62.)

I believe this incident strengthened Peter's commitment. He was never to be weak again. The resolve borne of that disappointment in his own temporary weakness tempered his metal into the hardest steel. He proved his devotion every day of his life thereafter, and in his death. So it can be with all of us. When we have been less than we ought to be and have fallen below our own standards, we can have newfound resolve and strength by forsaking our weakness.

God help us to be honest and true. May we always be thoroughly dependable, standing firm and upright though others may fail, and be fearless, constant, and just. May we say with the much tested Job: "Till I die I will not remove mine integrity from me." (Job 27:5.)

Chapter 9

"WILL I BE HAPPY?"

On the wall of a stake president's office in Brisbane, Australia, is the picture of a sad-faced little girl, and above it is this question: "Will I Be Happy?" I suppose everyone in the world could ask that question. The Savior himself prayed that all of his disciples "might have . . . joy fulfilled in themselves." (John 17:13.)

I have a hope that children will know a future filled with some happiness and peace. No gift bestowed upon us is so precious as children. They are proof that God still loves us. They are the hope of the future. In today's world, I cannot help wondering, Who will love them enough to help them be happy? Who will love them enough to teach them faith and moral values? They must learn so much more than survival and self-gratification. There is such a great need for the teaching of the heart and for the civilizing part of education. Where will children learn virtue? Who will care for them enough to mold their moral character? How can they become humane, kind, and happy and make life richer for themselves and others?

Teaching the next generation these values is not easy in a society where many fundamental beliefs are disappearing. Deadly worldly mores, often packaged attractively and mass marketed, today challenge almost every cherished human value. Excessive permissiveness under the banner of individual freedom is one driving force behind this. It is almost impossible to reach a public consensus on what values should be taught to the next generation. People strongly disagree about almost everything. Social restraints are weakened.

This means we must teach our children a life-style of our own and provide moral anchors in the sea of self-indulgence, self-interest, and self-service in which they float.

How can the tide of wrong values be reversed? Can anything be done to combat these challenges? May I suggest three ways to increase the hope that the next generation will grow up with a greater chance to find some continued happiness.

1. *Adults need to understand, and our children should be taught, that private choices are not private; they all have public consequences.*

There is a popular notion that doing our own thing or doing what feels good is our own business and affects no one but us. The deadly scourges that are epidemic all over the world have flourished in the context of this popular notion. But this is simply not true. All immoral behavior directly affects society. Even innocent people are affected. Drug and alcohol abuse have public consequences, as do illegitimacy, pornography, and obscenity. The public cost in human life and tax dollars for these so-called private choices is enormous: poverty, crime, a less-educated work force, and mounting demands for government spending to fix problems that cannot be fixed by money. It simply is not true that our private conduct is our own business. Our society is the sum total of what millions of individuals do in their private lives. That sum total of private behavior has worldwide public consequences of enormous magnitude. There are no completely private choices.

2. *Adults and children need to know that public and private morality is not outmoded.*

We need to love our children enough to teach them that laws, policies, and public programs with a moral and ethical basis are necessary for the preservation of a peaceful, productive, compassionate, and happy society. Without the qualities and characteristics of integrity, honesty, commitment, loyalty, respect for others, fidelity, and virtue, a free and open society cannot endure.

Elder Dallin H. Oaks recently responded to those who say, "Don't legislate morality." Said he: "I suppose persons who mouth that familiar slogan think they are saying something profound. In fact, if that is an argument at all, it is so superficial that an educated person should be ashamed to use it. As should be evident to every thinking person, a high proportion of all legislation has a moral base. That is true of the criminal law, most of the laws regulating family relations, businesses, and commercial transactions, many of the laws governing property, and a host of others." ("Gambling—Morally Wrong and Politically Unwise," address given at Ricks College, January 6, 1987.)

Until recently, ethics and moral philosophy were the foundation of higher education. They were a legacy passed from generation to generation. Those values are as relevant today as when they were taught by Aristotle, who said, "Man perfected by society is the best of all animals; he is the most terrible of all when he lives without law, and without justice." Therefore, public and private morality need much greater emphasis everywhere.

3. *We need to fortify the family.*

For centuries the family was the bedrock of this and many other nations. It was the glue that held society together. Now many families are in trouble, and the glue is coming unstuck.

As a result, many children are bewildered: they are growing physically but lack the support system, the disciplined moral framework, and the love and understanding that a strong family can provide. It is in a home and with a family that values are usually acquired, traditions are fostered, and commitments to others are established. There are really no adequate substitutes. Church, school, and government programs can only reinforce and supplement that which is acquired at home.

To strengthen the family, the morals of human sexuality need to be restored. One author wrote, "Children who have watched parents treat one another with affection and courtesy already understand more about the relationship between the sexes than they will ever learn from any class in reproductive physiology." (Bryce Christensen, *The Family in America*, March 1987, 1:3.)

The word of the Lord teaches that all men and women are to practice chastity before marriage and fidelity after marriage. "Thou shalt not commit adultery," he said (Exodus 20:14), "nor do anything like unto it" (D&C 59:6; see also 1 Corinthians 6:9 and Alma 39:1–13).

Alternatives to the legal and loving marriage between a man and a woman are helping to unravel the fabric of human society. That fabric, of course, is the family. These so-called alternative life-styles cannot be accepted as right because they frustrate God's commandment for a life-giving union of male and female within a legal marriage. (Genesis 1:28.) If practiced by all adults, such life-styles would mean the end of the family.

The scriptures clearly and consistently condemn all sex relations outside of legal marriage as morally wrong. Why is this so? It is so because God said so. It is so because we are made in the image of God, male and female. (Genesis 1:27.)

We are his spirit children. (D&C 76:24.) We were with him in the beginning. (D&C 93:23.) Bringing to pass our exaltation is his work and glory. (Moses 1:39.) We are directed to be the children of light. (D&C 106:5.) We are heirs to eternal life. The Spirit gives light to every person who comes into the world. (D&C 84:46.)

What values can be taught most effectively in the home? By commandment, parents in the Church are to teach their children faith in Christ, repentance, baptism, and the gift of the Holy Ghost. (D&C 68:25.) At home, in the warm security of discipline and love, we learn the values that never change. We learn the differences between right and wrong, as well as self-discipline, self-mastery, personal responsibility, all of the essentials of good character, concern for others, and civil manners. Values, public as well as private, cannot last very long without being regenerated and sustained by religious belief; they are a matter of continued renewal. An awakening of faith and belief in religious values is essential. Family teachings are encouraged by the Church, and the Church, in turn, through its covenants and ordinances, unifies the eternal family.

Some say families cannot do the job because so many people just do not have families. It is true that many individuals do not have a functioning family. It is also said that too many families fail. Unfortunately, that too is true. However, with all its shortcomings, the family is far and away the greatest social unit, the best answer to human problems, in the history of mankind. Rather than further weaken the family ties, we need to strengthen them. I urge overburdened parents to accept every help. Grandparents, brothers, sisters, aunts, uncles, cousins, and friends can also reinforce, by example and precept, their love and concern for members of the extended family.

My Aunt Angie has made 175 quilts for her children, grandchildren, nieces, nephews, and others. They are works of art; but more important, each is a labor of love. She can say to a member of her extended family, as she presents a specially made quilt, "Except when I pricked my finger, with every stitch I thought of my love for you."

Good family life seems to have little to do with whether we are in affluent or humble circumstances. All over the world are poor people who have good, resilient families. They do their best to raise children and be good neighbors; they are "money-poor" but "value-wealthy." Family problems seem to fall on both the wealthy and the impoverished.

The White House Conference on Families reports:

"For most . . . life is not a matter of legislative battles, judicial decrees and executive decisions. It is a fabric of helping hands and good neighbors; bedtime stories and shared prayers; loving-packed lunchboxes and household budget balancing; tears wiped away and a precious heritage passed along; it is hard work, and a little put away for the future. In a healthy society, heroes are the men, women, and children who hold the world together one home at a time; the parents and grandparents who forgo pleasures, delay purchases, foreclose options, and commit most of their lives to the noblest undertaking of citizenship; raising children who, resting on the shoulders of the previous generation, will see farther than we and reach higher. . . .

"Good families, rich or poor or in between, provide encouragement and support to their children, but no excuses. They teach character. They insist upon standards. They demand respect. They require performance." (*The White House Report on the Family,* November 1986, pp. 8–9, 32.)

Troubled as many homes in our society may be, we cannot abandon the home as the primary teacher of moral values.

Nowhere else will moral values be taught so effectively. As Brigham Young counseled, we must teach children "by faith rather than by the rod, leading them kindly by good example into all truth and holiness." (*Journal of Discourses* 12:174.)

There is a deep private and public need to retrieve for children the comfort of belief and of belonging. The products of wealth, technology, and science all fail to satisfy inner spiritual hungering.

Without turning back to the word of our Creator, no one is wise enough to sort out what ethical, spiritual, and moral values should be taught to the next generation, and to their children, and to their children's children.

There is reason for hope. More people today seem to be recognizing that public solutions are not so effective as family solutions. Some authority seems to be returning to the head of the home. But, most important, I see many adults, mostly parents and grandparents, who truly love children. If in the process we can bring back into our lives and into our homes sacred spiritual and moral truths, we will reclaim a sacred and precious part of our heritage.

Someone must love the children enough to do this. Then, if it is done everywhere, to the boys and girls who ask, "Will I be happy?" we can answer: "Of course! You are going to be happy, and even more. If you keep the covenants and commandments of God, you will have the joy promised by the Savior when he walked upon the earth. You will have 'peace in this world, and eternal life in the world to come.' " (D&C 59:23.)

Chapter 10

CARING FOR OURSELVES
AND OUR LOVED ONES

In 1936 the First Presidency said in a great statement of purpose, "The aim of the Church is to help the people to help themselves." (Conference Report, October 1936, p. 3.)

Many people today are children of the Great Depression of the 1930s. Most of us who passed through that period will never forget the difficult economic times almost everyone experienced. At that time many banks failed; people lost their life's savings; a great many were unemployed, and some lost their homes because they could not pay the mortgage. Many went hungry. If we didn't eat our oatmeal cereal for breakfast, we would often have it fried for lunch or dinner. Such widespread economic problems could come again. And any of us, at any time, could meet with a personal calamity, such as sickness or an accident, which could limit or destroy our income.

The purpose of the Church's welfare program is to care for the poor and the needy and make the Latter-day Saints, by their obedience to gospel principles, strong and self-reliant. At the center of caring for the poor and the needy in a world-wide church are a generous contribution to the fast offerings and personal and family preparedness. At the very heart of taking care of our own needs is our own energy and ability, with help to and from our own families.

I should like to discuss five prescriptions which, if followed, will make each of us better able to control our destinies.

First prescription: Practice thrift and frugality.

A wise old saying states, "Eat it up, wear it out, make it do, or do without." Thrift is a practice of not wasting anything. Some people are able to get by because of the absence of expense. They have their shoes resoled, they patch, they mend, they sew, and they save money. They avoid installment buying and make purchases only after saving enough to pay cash, thus avoiding interest charges.

The old couplet "Waste not, want not" still has much merit. Frugality requires that we live within our income and save a little for a rainy day, which always seems to come. It means avoiding debt and carefully limiting purchases on credit. It means learning to distinguish between wants and needs. It means exercising self-discipline to avoid the "buy now, pay later" philosophy, and adopting the practice of "save now and buy later." Some investment counselors urge speculative credit practices described as "leverage," "credit wealth," and "borrow yourself rich." Such practices may work successfully for some, but at best they succeed only for a time. An economic reversal always seems to come, and many who have followed such practices find themselves in financial ruin and their lives in shambles.

In a talk at Brigham Young University on February 28, 1963, President Ezra Taft Benson stated: "A large proportion of families with personal debt have no liquid assets whatsoever to fall back upon. What troubles they invite if their income should be suddenly cut off or seriously reduced! We all know of families who have obligated themselves for more than they could pay."

Owning a home free of debt is an important goal of provident living, although it may not be a realistic possibility for some. A mortgage on a home leaves a family unprotected against severe financial storms. Homes that are free and clear of mortgages and liens cannot be foreclosed on. When there are good financial times, it is the most opportune time to retire our debts and pay installments in advance. It is a truth that "the borrower is servant to the lender." (Proverbs 22:7.)

Many young people have become so hypnotized by the rhythm of monthly payments they scarcely think of the total cost of what they buy. They immediately want things it took their parents years to acquire. It is not the pathway to happiness to assume debts for a big home, an expensive car, or the most stylish clothes just so we can keep up with the Joneses. Payment of obligations is a sacred trust. Most of us will never be rich, but we can feel greatly unburdened when we are debt-free.

Second prescription: Seek to be independent.

The Lord said that it is important for the Church to "stand independent above all other creatures beneath the celestial world." (D&C 78:14.) Latter-day Saints are also counseled to be independent. Independence means many things. It means being free of drugs that addict, habits that bind, and diseases that curse. It also means being free of personal debt and of the interest and carrying charges required by debt the world over.

President J. Reuben Clark's classic statement on interest bears repeating: "Interest never sleeps nor sickens nor dies; it never goes to the hospital; it works on Sundays and holidays; it never takes a vacation; it never visits nor travels; it takes no pleasure; it is never laid off work nor discharged from employment; it never works on reduced hours; it never has short crops or droughts; it never pays taxes; it buys no food; it wears no clothes; it is unhoused and without home and so has no repairs, no replacements, no shingling, plumbing, painting, or whitewashing; it has neither wife, children, father, mother, nor kinfolk to watch over and care for; it has no expense of living; it has neither weddings nor births nor deaths; it has no love, no sympathy; it is as hard and soulless as a granite cliff. Once in debt, interest is your companion every minute of the day and night; you cannot shun it or slip away from it; you cannot dismiss it; it yields neither to entreaties, demands, or orders; and whenever you get in its way or cross its course or fail to meet its demands, it crushes you." (Conference Report, April 1938, p. 103.)

Extended economic dependence humiliates people if they are strong, and debilitates them if they are weak. Payment of our tithes and offerings can help us become independent. President Nathan Eldon Tanner said:

"Paying tithing is discharging a debt to the Lord. . . . If we obey this commandment, we are promised that we will 'prosper in the land.' This prosperity consists of more than material goods—it may include enjoying good health and vigor of mind. It includes family solidarity and spiritual increase." (Conference Report, October 1979, p. 119.)

I firmly believe, after many years of close observation, that those who honestly pay their tithes and offerings do prosper and get along better in almost every way. I testify that in discharging this debt to the Lord, we can enjoy great personal satisfaction. Unfortunately such satisfaction will be known only by those who have the faith and strength to keep this commandment.

Third prescription: Be industrious.

To be industrious involves energetically managing our circumstances to our advantage. It also means being enterprising and taking advantage of opportunities. Industry requires resourcefulness. A good idea can be worth years of struggle.

A friend who owned some fertile fields complained to his sister about his lack of means. "What about your crops?" asked the sister. The impoverished man replied, "There was so little snow in the mountains, I thought there would be a drought, so I did not plant." As it turned out, unforeseen spring rains made the crops bountiful for those industrious enough to plant. We deny the divinity within us when we doubt our potential and our possibilities. The great poet Virgil said, "They conquer who believe they can." Alma testified, speaking of a just God, "I know that he granteth unto men according to their desire." (Alma 29:4.)

To be industrious involves work. It involves creativity. It also involves rest. It includes both aspects of Sabbath day observance: we are to labor six days and we are to rest one day. This rest will leave us with more energy and resources to make the rest of the week more productive and fruitful.

Fourth prescription: Become self-reliant.

I have always admired those who have the ability and skills to make things with their hands. The ability to make repairs around the home, to improvise, to take care of our machinery, to keep our automobiles running, is not only an economic advantage but also provides much emotional resilience.

President Spencer W. Kimball counseled: "I hope that we understand that, while having a garden, for instance, is often useful in reducing food costs and making available delicious fresh fruits and vegetables, it does much more than this. Who can gauge the value of that special chat between daughter and Dad as they weed or water the garden? How do we evaluate the good that comes from the obvious lessons of planting, cultivating, and the eternal law of the harvest? And how do we measure the family togetherness and cooperating that must accompany successful canning? Yes, we are laying up resources in store, but perhaps the greater good is contained in the lessons of life we learn as we live providently and extend to our children their pioneer heritage." (Conference Report, October 1977, p. 125.) This heritage includes teaching our children how to work.

Fifth prescription: Strive to have a year's supply of food and clothing.

The counsel to have a year's supply of basic food, clothing, and commodities was given more than fifty years ago and has been repeated many times since. Fathers and mothers are the family's storekeepers. They should store whatever their own family needs to have in case of an emergency. Most of us cannot afford to store a year's supply of luxury items, but find it more practical to store staples that might keep us from starving in case of emergency. Surely we all hope that the hour of need will never come. Some have said, "We have followed this counsel in the past and have never had need to use our year's supply, so we have difficulty keeping this in mind as a major priority." Perhaps following this counsel could be the reason why they have not needed to use their reserve. Continued rotation of the supply can keep it usable with no waste.

The Church cannot be expected to provide for every one of its millions of members in case of public or personal disaster. It is therefore necessary that every home and family do what they can to assume responsibility for their own hour of need. If we do not have the resources to acquire a year's supply, then we can strive to begin with having one month's supply. I believe that if we are provident and wise in managing our personal and family affairs and are faithful, God will sustain us through our trials. He has revealed: "For the earth is full, and there is enough and to spare; yea, I prepared all things, and have given unto the children of men to be agents unto themselves." (D&C 104:17.)

Much of our well-being is bound up in caring for others. King Benjamin, speaking through the pages of the Book of Mormon, counsels, "I would that ye should impart of your substance to the poor, every man according to that which he hath, such as feeding the hungry, clothing the naked, visiting the sick and administering to their relief, both spiritually and temporally, according to their wants." (Mosiah 4:26.)

The parable of the ten virgins, five wise and five foolish, has both a spiritual and a temporal application. Each of us has a lamp to light the way, but we must put the oil in our own lamps to produce that light. It is not enough to sit idly by and say, "The Lord will provide." He has promised: "They that are wise and have received the truth, and have taken the Holy Spirit for their guide, . . . the earth shall be given unto them for an inheritance; and they shall multiply and wax strong, and their children shall grow up without sin unto salvation.

"For the Lord shall be in their midst, and his glory shall be upon them, and he will be their king and their lawgiver." (D&C 45:57–59.)

Chapter 11

MEETING THE CHALLENGES
OF ECONOMIC STRESS

Some years ago Bishop James T. Erekson, a wise and successful member of a high council on which I served, made a statement that impressed me greatly. He said, "There are many in our generation who have not known the blessings of economic adversity!"

Economists seem to have a hard time deciding when we are in a depression or a recession. One person said you can tell it this way: "A recession: a period in which you tighten your belt. A depression: a time in which you have no belt to tighten." (*Braude Speakers' Encyclopedia*, p. 46.)

Many countries of the world have moved into more difficult times. Some people are losing their employment and their hard-earned possessions. Others are faced with lack of food and clothing. In a normal lifetime most people have had, or will face, difficult economic times. We read in Ecclesiastes 9:11 that "the race is not to the swift, nor the battle to the strong, neither yet bread to the wise, nor yet riches to men of understanding, nor yet favour to men of skill; but time and chance happeneth to them all."

The Savior verified this when, speaking of the Father, he said, "He maketh his sun to rise on the evil and on the good, and sendeth rain on the just and on the unjust." (Matthew 5:45.)

There are lessons from the dispensations of the gospel that help us understand that some calamities are ultimately blessings. Although the following examples have far greater meaning for mankind in general, they have lessons for us individually when we are confronted with trials in our lives.

The great suffering of the Savior in Gethsemane and his crucifixion were calamities, but man was redeemed from death and hell by his atoning sacrifice. The scattering of Israel throughout the world sprinkled the blood that believes, so that many nations may now partake of the gospel plan. The history of the Nephites is one of trial, calamities, and suffering, but through it all the experiences gained brought strength and development.

The Lord knows the values to be learned from trials and adversities.

Every year is a year for new opportunities. Charles Dickens laid the setting for his book *A Tale of Two Cities* in the following introduction: "It was the best of times, it was the worst of times, it was the age of wisdom, it was the age of foolishness, it was the epoch of belief, it was the epoch of incredulity, it was the season of Light, it was the season of Darkness, it was the spring of hope, it was the winter of despair, we had everything before us, we had nothing before us."

Aside from the economic tides that run in the affairs of nations, financial hard times can befall any of us at any time. There is no guarantee against personal hard financial times. Financial difficulty may result from many kinds of misfortunes, including natural disasters such as floods, fires, and earthquakes. Accidents and illness can produce unexpected and staggering medical and hospital bills. The misfortunes of other members of our own family may require our help. Unemployment and inflation can quickly wipe away hard-earned savings.

Economic stress can involve personal challenges. Discouragement and frustration are frequent companions to misfortune. Economic problems occasionally put a strain on family relationships. They often require that we do without things we feel we want or need. What is a calamity for one may be an opportunity for another. Shakespeare, speaking through Duke Senior, said, "Sweet are the uses of adversity, / Which, like the toad, ugly and venomous, / Wears yet a precious jewel in his head." (*As You Like It,* Act 2, sc. 1.)

The lasting effects of economic challenges are often determined by our attitude toward life. One observer wrote: "Out of the same substances one stomach will extract nourishment, and another poison; and so the same disappointments in life will chasten and refine one man's spirit and embitter another's." (William Matthews, *Webster's Encyclopedia of Dictionaries,* Ottenheimer Publishers, Inc., p. 864.)

Elder LeGrand Richards told this story to a young person who in a time of desperation asked what youth have to live for: "You remember the story of the two buckets that went down in the well; as the one came up, it said, 'This is surely a cold and dreary world. No matter how many times I come up full, I always have to go down empty.' Then the other bucket laughed and said, 'With me it is different. No matter how many times I go down empty, I always come up full.' " (Conference Report, April 1951, p. 40.)

Brother Joseph Stucki, a faithful Church member, died on Christmas Eve in 1927 after a short illness, leaving his wife with seven children, the eldest son being on a mission. Two of the children and a nephew she was rearing were later taken in death. Another son also went on a mission. This was accomplished by much hard work—taking in sewing and living on a few dollars a month from an insurance policy.

During this difficult time, flour was being distributed to needy members of the ward. Some of the young men were asked to deliver it. A bag of flour was brought to Sister Stucki's home. Since she felt that other families in the ward needed that flour worse than she did, she declined to keep it, telling the young man that she was trying to teach her family to be independent and self-reliant. While worthy members of the Church should feel free to accept help from the Church proffered by the bishop, Sister Stucki was trying to teach the young man who came to her door a lesson. You see, the young man delivering the flour was her own son. All the surviving children attended college and became very successful people. They lived by the motto "Make it do, or do without."

Some of the blessings available when one overcomes economic adversity are:

First, and perhaps most important, our faith and testimony can be strengthened. The faithful Latter-day Saint learns that in times of economic stress, the Lord helps those who have sought him early. (See D&C 54:10.) But those who haven't begun early in their religious life may resolve to seek the Lord more diligently. Through adversity we learn to recognize the Lord's hand in helping us. In hard times we have a chance to reevaluate and reorder our priorities in life. We learn what is most important to us. The way is open to strengthen faith and testimony.

Second, we may learn the need for humility. Our dependence upon the Lord becomes a means of developing teachableness, an important aspect of humility.

Third, family members learn cooperation and love for one another by being forced to draw closer together to survive.

Fourth, personal dignity and self-respect may be achieved. Someone said, "Be glad there are big hurdles in life, and rejoice, too, that they are higher than most people care to surmount. Be happy they are numerous."

Fifth, we can become stronger and more resilient. Edmund Burke said: "Difficulty is a severe instructor, set over us by the supreme ordinance of a parental Guardian and Legislator, who knows us better than we know ourselves, he loves us better too. . . . He that wrestles with us strengthens our nerves, and sharpens our skill. Our antagonist is our helper."

Sixth, we learn patience. Sometimes economic adversity requires more time than we anticipate. Those who learn to bear their adversities while working to overcome them increase in patience, and thus they are not overcome by their circumstances. In economic and social affliction certain people of the Book of Mormon were exhorted to bear them patiently, that they "not be led away by the temptations of the devil." (Alma 34:39.)

Seventh, we rise to heights previously unobtainable by the use of talents and skills that might not have been developed otherwise. Economic necessity opens the way for profitable learning experiences.

Eighth, we can learn to trust the Lord and thus overcome fear. "If ye are prepared ye shall not fear." (D&C 38:30.)

There are many ways economic hard times can be met. Sometimes we must accept less than we hope for. A speaker once stated, "I passed a small church displaying a large sign. It read: 'Annual Strawberry Festival,' and below in small letters 'On account of depression, prunes will be served.' " (*Braude Speakers' Encyclopedia*, p. 51.)

Karen Nielson was born in Aalborg, Denmark, in 1844, the daughter of a farm family. In her early years she was taught the skills of dairy farming by her father. In 1861, Karen was baptized into The Church of Jesus Christ of Latter-day Saints and was never able to return to her home because of her father's opposition to her conversion. She left Denmark and immigrated to Utah with a group of Scandinavian Saints in 1862. She lived for a few years in Utah County, where she married Benjamin Franklin Barney, and then they were called to settle the Sevier Valley.

Karen bore ten children and then was left a widow with several of her children still at home. She had no close family to return to, so she drew on the knowledge she had gained on the Danish farm. She improved her dairy herd using the breeding skills she'd learned from her father. Her herd was soon recognized as one of the finest in the area, and she was able to support her family and care for their needs. Until Karen was well into her eighties, she milked her cows morning and night and cared for her farm with the help of her sons and grandsons. Her legacy was one of hard work and the knowledge that our lives are only as good as we make them. She never turned away from hardships—they seemed only to strengthen her.

I have previously suggested eight blessings that may come as we strive to overcome economic adversities. I should now like to suggest six ways to help us from being overcome by economic stress:

1. *Seek first the kingdom of God.* (See Matthew 6:33.)

This seeking includes the payment of our tithes and a generous fast offering and thus being blessed both spiritually and temporally by our obedience. Seeking first the kingdom of God involves striving to keep the law the Apostle James called the "the royal law," which is "Thou shalt love thy neighbour as thyself." (James 2:8.) Seeking first the kingdom of God involves keeping the divine commandments. Spiritual strength comes from many sources, including personal prayer, studying the scriptures, and the willingness to "submit to all things which the Lord seeth fit to inflict." (Mosiah 3:19.) These measures can give us a certain, peaceful stability.

2. *Solidify family strengths and resources.*

Chief among a family's resources are its spiritual strengths, which are enhanced by praying together. Budgeting money together will produce a special unity, as will the holding of family councils. We should work together toward storing a year's supply of food, clothing, and other necessities. In times of stress extra acts of kindness are particularly needed and appreciated. When there is limited money available, it is easier to teach children the wise use of money, including the need to save for the future. The family can be reminded to maintain an eternal perspective rather than concentrate on worldly possessions and wealth. Family organizations are helpful to render the individual help that may be needed. It is also important to learn how to accept family help graciously.

3. *Exercise faith.*

The Savior reminds us, "All things are possible to him that believeth" (Mark 9:23), and "All things shall work together for your good" (D&C 90:24). The attitude with which we submit to "all things" is important. Maintaining a positive attitude and being cheerful are helpful. A belief that "all these things shall give thee experience, and shall be for thy good" is like a spiritual stabilizer. (D&C 122:7.)

4. *Be adaptable in your work.*

Theodore Roosevelt said: "No man needs sympathy because he has to work. . . . Far and away the best prize that life offers is the chance to work hard at work worth doing." In times of economic difficulty it may be necessary to work for less pay. We should be willing to learn new, marketable skills. Many people have found new joy and satisfaction in having a second career wholly unrelated to the work for which they were originally trained. Family members need to find ways to supplement income through appropriate work opportunities. Being flexible in our approach to such opportunities may just make it possible to keep afloat financially. Giving a full day's work for a full day's pay has saved many jobs. It will also help us avoid accepting government doles that rob us of our dignity and our self-respect.

5. *Avoid debt.*

President J. Reuben Clark, Jr., taught us to "avoid debt as we would a plague." (Conference Report, April 1937, p. 26.) This is particularly sound counsel in these times of exorbitantly high interest rates. Debt and interest are merciless taskmasters.

6. *Reduce expense.*

When asked how some people in a small farming community in southern Utah got by on meager cash income, George Lyman said, "They lived on the absence of expense." Humorist Sam Levenson once observed, "Generations of great thinkers have dreamed of a moneyless society somewhere in the future. As far as some of us are concerned, we're already ahead of our time." Economic wealth does not endow eternal blessings, and financial difficulty does not revoke eternal covenants.

Elder Neal A. Maxwell said: "An economic depression would be grim, but it would not change the reality of immortality. The inevitability of the second coming is not affected by the unpredictability of the stock market. . . . A case of cancer does not cancel the promise of the temple endowment. . . . All that matters is gloriously intact. The promises are in place. It is up to us to perform." (*Notwithstanding My Weakness,* Salt Lake City: Deseret Book, 1981, p. 57.)

Before teaching the parable of the rich man whose ground

brought forth plentifully, Jesus said, "Take heed, and beware of covetousness: for a man's life consisteth not in the abundance of the things which he possesseth." (Luke 12:15.)

The Lord has said: "Trouble me no more concerning this matter. But learn that he who doeth the works of righteousness shall receive his reward, even peace in this world, and eternal life in the world to come." (D&C 59:22–23.)

From the refiner's fire of economic difficulty may come eternal blessings that can help save families and exalt their members by uniting and strengthening them.

Chapter 12

COMFORT AND
HOPE FOR FAMILIES

It is a common sight in our congregations to have a small group of people near the front who communicate by the graceful motion of the hands as well as by the spirit. They are people who cannot hear. Always some kind and gifted soul sits in front of the group and lovingly converts the sounds and syllables into distinguishable motions.

Recently in a large meeting, we were touched to observe the hearing-impaired members singing the hymns in parts through the motion of their hands. When the bass and tenor parts were sung, the hands of the sisters were motionless; when the soprano and alto parts were sung, the hands of the brethren were still. To me it was a very touching sight.

Those who are without hearing are some of the special ones among us, as are persons who do not have sight and persons who have other physical or mental limitations.

I wish to say a word of appreciation for those among us who struggle with handicaps, and impart a message of comfort to their families, especially to the parents. Where in all of the world is there a son or a daughter of God who is totally without blemish? Is life not worth living if it is not perfect? Do not the people with handicaps also bring their own gifts to life—and to others who are free of those handicaps—in a manner that cannot come in any other way? There is hardly a family without one member who might be considered physically or mentally diminished. I have great appreciation for those loving parents who stoically bear and overcome their anguish and heartbreak for a child who was born with or who has developed a serious mental or physical infirmity. This anguish often continues every day, without relief, during the lifetime of the parent or the child. Not infrequently, parents are required to give superhuman nurturing care that never ceases, day or night. Many a mother's arms and heart have ached years on end, giving comfort and relieving the suffering of her special child.

The anguish of parents upon first learning that their child is not developed normally can be indescribable. The tearful concern, the questions about what the child will and will not be able to do are heartrending: "Doctor, will our child be able to talk, walk, care for himself?" Often there are no certain answers but one: "You will have to be grateful for whatever development your child achieves."

The paramount concern is always how to care for the person who is handicapped. The burden of future nurturing can seem overwhelming. Looking ahead to the uncertain years or even to a lifetime of constant care may seem more than one can bear. Often many tears are shed before reality is acknowledged. Parents and family members can then begin to accept and take the burden one day at a time.

Said one mother of a severely handicapped child, "I gradually began to take only one day at a time, and it didn't seem so hard. In fact, at the end of each day I would thank the Lord for the strength I had to get through that day and pray that tomorrow would be as good. That way I learned to love my son and appreciate his place in our home."

A missionary writing to his parents said of his severely handicapped younger brother, "Mom, kiss Billy every day for me. In one of the discussions we learned that my little brother is an automatic winner of the kingdom of God. I only pray that I too may live with my Heavenly Father and see my little brother and talk and converse with him. He's a special gift, and we are truly blessed."

The challenge of having handicapped people is not new. Many have questioned why some have such limitations. It was so in the time of Jesus. "And as Jesus passed by, he saw a man which was blind from his birth. And his disciples asked him, saying, Master, who did sin, this man, or his parents, that he was born blind? Jesus answered, Neither hath this man sinned, nor his parents: but that the works of God should be made manifest in him." (John 9:1–3.)

How are the works of God manifested in these, our handicapped brothers and sisters? Surely they are manifested greatly in the loving care and attention given by parents, other family members, friends, and associates. The handicapped are not on trial. Those of us who live free of such limitations are the ones who are on trial. While those with handicaps cannot be measured in the same way as others, many of the handicapped benefit immensely from each accomplishment, no matter how small.

The handiwork of God is manifested with respect to the handicapped in many ways. It is demonstrated in the miraculous ways in which many individuals with mental and physical impediments are able to adjust and compensate for their limitations. Occasionally, other senses become more functional and substitute for the impaired senses in a remarkable way. A young friend greatly retarded in speech and movement repaired a complicated clock although she had had no previous training or experience in watch or clock making.

Many of the special ones are superior in many ways. They, too, are in a life of progression, and new things unfold for them each day as with us all. They can be extraordinary in their faith and spirit. Some are able, through prayer, to communicate with the infinite in a most remarkable way. Many have a pure faith in others and a powerful belief in God. They can give their spiritual strength to others around them.

For those who are impaired, trying to cope with life is often like trying to reach the unreachable. But recall the words of the Prophet Joseph Smith: "All the minds and spirits that God ever sent into the world are susceptible of enlargement." (*Teachings of the Prophet Joseph Smith,* p. 354.) Certainly, in the infinite mercy of God, those with physical and mental limitations will not remain so after the Resurrection. At that time, Alma says, "the spirit and the body shall be reunited again in perfect form; both limb and joint shall be restored to its proper frame." (Alma 11:43.) Afflictions, like mortality, are temporary.

Surely more sharing of the burden will contribute to the emotional salvation of the person who is the primary caregiver. Just an hour of help now and then would be appreciated. One mother of a child who is handicapped said, "I could never dream of going to Hawaii on a vacation; all I can hope for is to have an evening away from home."

The Savior's teachings that handicaps are not punishment for sin, either in the parents or in the handicapped, can also be understood and applied in today's circumstances. How can it possibly be said that an innocent child born with a special problem is being punished? Why should parents who have kept themselves free from social disease, addicting chemicals, and other debilitating substances that might affect their offspring imagine that the birth of a disabled child is some form of divine disapproval? Usually, both the parents are blameless. The Savior of the world reminds us that God "maketh his sun to rise on the evil and on the good, and sendeth rain on the just and on the unjust." (Matthew 5:45.)

May I express a word of gratitude and appreciation to those many who minister with such kindness and skill to our handicapped people. Special commendation belongs to parents and family members who have cared for their own children with special needs in the loving atmosphere of their own homes. The care of those who are diminished is a special service rendered to the Master himself, for "inasmuch as ye have done it unto one of the least of these my brethren, ye have done it unto me." (Matthew 25:40.)

Parents of handicapped children are occasionally embarrassed or hurt by others who awkwardly express sympathy but cannot know or appreciate the depth of the parents' love for a handicapped child. Perhaps there is some comparison in the fact that there is no less love in families for the helpless infant who must be fed, bathed, and diapered than for older but still dependent members. We love those whom we serve and who need us.

Is it not possible to look beyond the canes, the wheelchairs, the braces, and the crutches into the hearts of the people who have need of these aids? They are human beings and want only to be treated as ordinary people. They may appear different, move awkwardly, speak haltingly, but they have the same feelings. They laugh, they cry, they know discouragment and hope. They do not want to be shunned. They want to be loved for what they are inside, without any prejudice for their impairment. Can there not be more tolerance for differences – differences in capacity, differences in body and in mind?

Those who are close to the handicapped can frequently

feel the nobility of the spirits who are confined in differently shaped bodies or who have crippled minds.

May I also offer a word of comfort for the anguished parents of children who have lost their way and have turned a deaf ear to parental pleading and teaching. While most of the time children follow in their parents' footsteps—obedient to their teachings, reciprocating their love—a few, like the prodigal son, turn their backs and waste their lives. The great principle of free agency is essential in fostering development, growth, and progress. It also permits the freedom to choose self-indulgence, wastefulness, and degradation. Children have their agency, and they may or may not follow the teachings and wishes of their parents. Most parents do the best they know how, but they also understand well the words of Lehi: "Hear the words of a trembling parent." (2 Nephi 1:14.)

We are indebted to Elder Howard W. Hunter for these wise words: "A successful parent is one who has loved, one who has sacrificed, and one who has cared for, taught, and ministered to the needs of a child. If you have done all of these and your child is still wayward or troublesome or worldly, it could well be that you are, nevertheless, a successful parent. Perhaps there are children who have come into the world that would challenge any set of parents under any set of circumstances. Likewise, perhaps there are others who would bless the lives of, and be a joy to, almost any father or mother." (*Ensign,* November 1983, p. 65.)

As caring parents we do the best we can. I am hopeful that God will judge parents at least partially by the intent of their hearts. Children have so much to learn. Parents need to teach their children so many things. They are commanded to teach their children specifically "the doctrine of repentance, faith in Christ the Son of the living God, and of baptism and the gift of the Holy Ghost by the laying on of the hands, when eight years old." (D&C 68:25.) But, having lived by these truths and having taught them in their home, parents cannot always ensure their children's good behavior. Said Ezekiel, "The son shall not bear the iniquity of the father, neither shall the father bear the iniquity of the son." (Ezekiel 18:20.)

Parents have the obligation to teach, not force, and having prayerfully and conscientiously taught, they cannot be answerable for all their children's conduct. Obedient children do bring honor to their parents, but it is unfair to judge faithful parents by the actions of children who will not listen and follow. Parents do have the obligation to instruct, but children themselves have a responsibility to listen, to be obedient, and to perform as they have been taught. Parents are parents, and usually they serve their children more than the children serve them. To concerned parents I would paraphrase Winston Churchill: "Never give up, never give up, never, never, never."

I do not have any foolproof formula for the nurturing of children. Beyond being a good example and teaching faith, it is essential to give children unreserved love, to give measured discipline, and to try to instill self-mastery in them. A mother who scrubbed floors to help her children through school said, "I taught my children to pray, to have good manners, and to work."

The works of God are manifested in many ways in the challenges of parents and children, especially to those who are handicapped and to those who have lost their way. For those who ask, "Why did this happen to my child?" there is assurance that the difficulty will not last forever. Life on this earth is not long. Caring for the unfortunate and laboring with the wayward are manifestations of the pure love of Christ. For those who carry such challenges in this life, God himself provides a response. That response is patience and strength to endure. It lies, as Paul and Job testify, "in hope of eternal life, which God . . . promised before the world began" (Titus 1:2), "when the morning stars sang together, and all the sons of God shouted for joy" (Job 38:7).

Chapter 13

ENRICHING
OUR FAMILY LIFE

As a young man I recall President J. Reuben Clark pleading time after time in general priesthood meetings that there be unity in the priesthood. He would quote frequently the message of the Lord, "I say unto you, be one; and if ye are not one ye are not mine." (D&C 38:27.)

Unity in the priesthood should reflect unity in our homes. One wonders why so many homes are now being weakened and why so many families are disintegrating. The reasons are complex. No doubt it has much to do with the social disorders of the day. We are all subjected to sparkling, enticing false advertising. Violence is powerfully portrayed everywhere. Our society is permeated with suggestions that selfishness and instant gratification are acceptable or even respectable conduct. The evils of alcoholism have exploded and been magnified by the other forms of drug abuse. The sexual revolution has been crippling to the spiritual, mental, and physical health of families.

Among the assaults on families are attacks on our faith. Some of this is coming from apostates who formerly had testimonies and now seem unable to leave the Church alone. One, complaining of Church policy, was heard to say, "I am so mad: if I had been paying tithing I would quit." Persecution is not new to devoted followers of Christ. More recently, however, the anger and venom of our enemies seems to be increasing. Brigham Young said, "We never begin to build a temple without the bells of hell beginning to ring." (*Discourses of Brigham Young,* p. 410.) With many temples under construction or in the planning stage, there seem to be a lot of bells to be rung.

When I hear of a family breaking up, I question if family home evening and family prayers have been regularly held in that home and if the law of tithing has been observed. Has that family reverenced the Sabbath day? Have the parents murmured against gospel teachings and Church leaders? I wonder what could possibly justify the forsaking of eternal promises made in the temple, or what could warrant the breaking up of a family with children of tender years. Why is one family strong, yet another family weak? The problems are infinitely complex. Yet, there are answers. Abundant evidence shows that the presence of a firm, loving father in the home is far more likely to produce responsible, law-abiding children than if the father is not there, or if he does not function as a father at home. Malachi said the whole world would be smitten with a curse if the hearts of the fathers were not turned to the children, and if the hearts of the children were not turned to their fathers. (See Malachi 4:6.)

Stable, strong families are more likely if the father is present in the home, one or both of the parents are active in the Church, and there is discipline in the home.

Surely, the most important ingredient in producing family happiness for members of the Church is a deep religious commitment under wise, mature parental supervision. Devotion to God seems to forge the spiritual moorings and stability that can help the family cope. Some may say this is an oversimplification of a very complex problem, yet I believe the answers lie within the framework of the restored gospel of Christ.

One of the reasons for weakened families is the lack of absolutes. An absolute has no restriction, exception, or qualification. It is fixed and certain. There must be some things that family members should always try to do, and some activities that family members should scrupulously avoid. Truthfulness should be an absolute in every family.

How can parents and family members introduce and build familial strength? One of my closest boyhood friends died of cancer some time ago. His family decided he would be happier spending his last days in his own home, so they took him out of the hospital where the cancer was diagnosed and cared for him within the familiar walls of his own house. His eighty-one-year-old mother left her home in another state and moved in to supervise the tender, loving care. A sister and a brother left their homes in distant areas several times to help in emergencies. His children, some of whom also lived away, came and set up a twenty-four-hour vigil so that he would never be alone. After a few months he passed away, wasted and emaciated, but contented and happy. He had been loved into death. The family could have left his care to the government and the hospital, with little expense and little personal inconvenience being involved, but they chose to do otherwise.

May I suggest other ways to enrich family life:

1. *Hold family prayer night and morning.* The source of our enormous individual strength and potential is no mystery. It is an endowment from God. We need not consume addicting chemicals found in drugs, including alcohol, to make us capable of meeting life's problems. We need only to draw constantly from the power source through humble prayer. Sometimes it takes a superhuman effort for parents of a busy family to get everyone out of bed and together for family prayer and

scripture study. You may not always feel like praying when you finally get together, but it will pay great dividends if you persevere.

2. *Study the scriptures.* We all need the strength that comes from daily reading of the scriptures. Parents must have a knowledge of the standard works in order to teach them to their children. A child who has been taught from the scriptures has a priceless legacy. Children are fortified when they become acquainted with the heroic figures and stories of the scriptures, such as Daniel in the lion's den, David and Goliath, Nephi, and Helaman and the stripling warriors. Having prayer, scripture study, and meals together provides important time for parents and children, brothers and sisters to talk and listen.

3. *Teach children to work.* Every household has routine daily chores that children can be responsible for. Such chores can teach them how to work and also give them a sense of importance in the family.

4. *Teach discipline and obedience.* If parents do not discipline their children and teach them to obey, society may discipline them in a way neither the parents nor the children will like. Dr. Lee Salk, child psychologist, said, "The 'do your own thing' trend has interfered with people developing close and trusting family relationships. It tells people that they are neurotic if they feel a sense of responsibility for the feelings of other family members. People are also told to let all their feelings out, even if it is very hurtful to someone else." (*U.S. News and World Report,* June 16, 1980, p. 60.) As Dr. Salk says, this is patently wrong. Without discipline and obedience in the home, the unity of the family collapses.

5. *Place a high priority on loyalty to each other. Loyal* has been defined as being "constant and faithful in any relation implying trust or confidence; bearing true allegiance to the con-

97

stituted authority." If family members are not loyal to each other, they cannot be loyal to themselves.

6. *Teach principles of self-worth and self-reliance.* One of the main problems in families today is that we spend less and less time together. Some spend an extraordinary amount of time, when they are together, in front of the television, which robs them of personal time for reinforcing feelings of self-worth.

Time together is precious time—time to talk, to listen, to encourage, and to show how to do things. Less time together can result in loneliness, which may produce inner feelings of being unsupported, not valued, and inadequate. Self-worth is reinforced in many ways. When parents say to a son or daughter, leaving the home for some activity, the simple but meaningful words, "Remember who you are," they have helped that child feel important.

7. *Develop family traditions.* Some of the strengths of families can be found in their own traditions, which may consist of such things as making special occasions of the blessing of children, baptisms, ordinations to the priesthood, birthdays, fishing trips, skits on Christmas Eve, family home evening, and so forth. The traditions of each family are unique and are important in establishing in each member a sense of belonging and of unity.

8. *Do everything in the spirit of love.* Elder LeGrand Richards shared with us the tender relationship he had with his father. Said he, "I walked into my father's apartment when he was just about ninety, . . . and as I opened the door, he stood up and walked toward me and took me in his arms and hugged and kissed me. He always did that. . . . Taking me in his arms and calling me by my kid name, he said, 'Grandy, my boy, I love you.' " (Conference Report, October 1967, pp. 111–12.)

Some parents find it difficult to express their love physically or vocally. I do not ever recall my own father using the words "Son, I love you," but he showed it in a thousand ways that were more eloquent than words. He rarely missed a practice, a game, a race, or any activity in which his sons participated.

The touch and time of the mother in the home makes that home warm, comfortable, and pleasant. Our wives and mothers deserve special support. President George Albert Smith, addressing husbands and fathers at a missionary conference in 1941, said: "Some seem to think that the woman's responsibility is to take care of the home and everything else while the man goes to meetings. I want to tell you that your chief responsibility is in your own home." This was confirmed by President Harold B. Lee, who told the priesthood, "The greatest of the Lord's work you brethren will ever do as fathers will be within the walls of your own home." (Conference Report, April 1973, p. 130.)

Let there be no ill will or anger between parents and children, brothers and sisters, and kinsmen. Lingering feelings of hurt or disagreement should be settled quickly. Why wait until one party is dying or dead?

May the rich humanness of warm, loving family life be restored and prevail in all our kinship. And may we put our lives and homes in order. We must stay true to the great absolutes of the restored gospel: namely, our Savior, Jesus Christ; the divine restoration of the gospel in our time; the truthfulness of the Book of Mormon; Joseph Smith's divine calling as a prophet of God; and continuing revelation to Joseph's successors, according to the needs of the Church and its members.

If we are united and go forward under the leadership of those who have the keys to the kingdom of God on earth, our homes will be enriched, our lives will be purified, and the gates of hell will not prevail against us. May we follow the counsel of Alma and "stand as witnesses of God at all times and in all things, and in all places that [we] may be in, even until death." (Mosiah 18:9.)

Chapter 14

"THE GREAT IMITATOR"

You may have heard the story of the disruptive boys in a Sunday School class who were asked by their exasperated teacher why they bothered to attend Sunday School. One of the more impudent boys replied, "We came to see you perform a miracle." The teacher walked over to the boy and responded, "We don't perform miracles here, but we do cast out devils!"

The devil and his angels are the source and mainspring of all evil. I think we will witness increasing evidence of Satan's power as the kingdom of God grows stronger. I believe his ever-expending efforts are some proof of the truthfulness of the work of the Church. In the future the opposition will be both more subtle and more open. It will be masked in greater sophistication and cunning, but it will also be more blatant. We will need greater spirituality to perceive all forms of evil and greater strength to resist it. But the disappointments and setbacks to the work of God will be temporary, for the work will go forward. (See D&C 65:2.)

It is not good practice to become intrigued by Satan and his mysteries. No good can come from getting close to evil. Like playing with fire, it is too easy to get burned. The only safe course is to keep well distanced from him and any of his wicked activities or nefarious practices. We should avoid at all cost the mischief of devil worship, sorcery, casting spells, witchcraft, voodooism, black magic, and other forms of demonism. However, Brigham Young said that it is important to "study . . . evil, and its consequences." (*Discourses of Brigham Young,* pp. 256–57.) Since Satan is the author of all evil in the world, it would therefore be essential to realize that he is the influence behind the opposition to the work of God. Alma stated the issue succinctly: "Whatsoever is good cometh from God, and whatsoever is evil cometh from the devil." (Alma 5:40.)

My principal reason for discussing this subject is to help our young people by warning them, as Paul said, "lest Satan should get an advantage of us: for we are not ignorant of his devices." (2 Corinthians 2:11.) We hope that they, unfamiliar with the sophistries of the world, can keep themselves free of Satan's enticements and deceitful ways. I personally claim no special insight into Satan's methods, but I have at times been able to identify his influence and his actions in my life and in the lives of others. When I was on my mission, Satan sought to divert me from my future path and, if possible, to destroy my usefulness in the Lord's work. That was almost fifty years ago, and I still remember how reasonable his entreaties seemed.

Who has not heard and felt the enticings of the devil? His voice often sounds reasonable and his message easy to justify. It is an enticing, intriguing voice with dulcet tones. It is neither hard nor discordant. No one would listen to Satan's voice if it sounded harsh or mean. If the devil's voice were unpleasant, it would not entice people to listen to it.

Shakespeare wrote, "The prince of darkness is a gentleman" (*King Lear,* Act 3, sc. 4), and "the devil can cite Scripture for his purpose" (*The Merchant of Venice,* Act 1, sc. 3). As the great deceiver, Lucifer has marvelous powers of deception. Paul said to the Corinthians, "No marvel; for Satan himself is transformed into an angel of light." (2 Corinthians 11:14; see also 2 Nephi 9:9.)

Some of Satan's most appealing lines are "Everyone does it," "If it doesn't hurt anybody else, it's all right," "If you feel all right about it, it's okay," and "It's the 'in' thing to do." These subtle entreaties make Satan the great imitator, the master deceiver, the arch counterfeiter, the great forger.

We all have an inner braking system that will stop us before we follow Satan too far down the wrong road. It is the still, small voice that is within us. But once we have succumbed, the braking system begins to leak brake fluid and our stopping mechanism becomes weak and ineffective.

The prince of darkness is often in very good company and can be found everywhere. Job said, "Again there was a day when the sons of God came to present themselves before the Lord, and Satan came also among them to present himself before the Lord. And the Lord said unto Satan, From whence comest thou? And Satan answered the Lord, and said, From going to and fro in the earth, and from walking up and down in it." (Job 2:1–2.)

Nephi has given us the pattern or formula by which Satan operates: "Others will he pacify, and lull them away into carnal security, that they will say: All is well in Zion; yea, Zion prospereth, all is well—and thus the devil cheateth their souls, and leadeth them away carefully down to hell. And behold, others he flattereth away, and telleth them there is no hell; and he saith unto them: I am no devil, for there is none—and thus he whispereth in their ears, until he grasps them with his awful chains, from whence there is no deliverance." (2 Nephi 28:21–22.)

The First Presidency described Satan: "He is working under such perfect disguise that many do not recognize either him or his methods. There is no crime he would not commit, no debauchery he would not set up, no plague he would not send, no heart he would not break, no life he would not take, no soul he would not destroy. He comes as a thief in the night; he is a wolf in sheep's clothing." (*Messages of the First Presidency,* comp. James R. Clark, Salt Lake City: Bookcraft, 1965–75, 6:179.)

Satan is the world's master in the use of flattery, and he knows the great power of speech. In the Book of Mormon we read that "he was learned, that he had a perfect knowledge of the language of the people; wherefore, he could use much flattery, and much power of speech, according to the power of the devil." (Jacob 7:4.) He has always been one of the great forces of the world.

Ernest LeRoy Hatch, former president of the Guatemala City Temple, said, "The devil is not smart because he is the devil; he is smart because he is old." Indeed, the devil is old, and he was not always the devil. Initially he was not the perpetrator of evil. He was with the hosts of heaven in the beginning. He was "an angel of God who was in authority in the presence of God." (D&C 76:25.) He came before Christ and proposed to God the Father, "Behold, here am I, send me, I will be thy son, and I will redeem all mankind, that one soul shall not be lost, and surely I will do it; wherefore give me thine honor." (Moses 4:1.) This he proposed to do by force, destroying the free agency of man.

Does his statement "Give me thine honor" mean that he wanted to mount an insurrection to supplant even God the Father? Satan became the devil by seeking glory, power, and dominion by force. (See Moses 4:3–4.) But Jesus, "chosen from the beginning," said unto God, "Father, thy will be done, and the glory be thine forever." (Moses 4:2.) What a contrast in approaches! Wrong as his plan was, Satan was persuasive enough to entice one-third of the hosts of heaven to follow him. He practiced a great deception by saying, "I am also a son of God." (Moses 5:13.)

Free agency, given us through the plan of our Father, is the great alternative to Satan's plan of force. With this sublime gift, we can grow, improve, progress, and seek perfection. Without agency, none of us could grow and develop by learning from our mistakes and errors and the mistakes and errors of others.

Because of his rebellion, Lucifer was cast out and became Satan, the devil, "the father of all lies, to deceive and to blind men, and to lead them captive at his will, even as many as would not hearken unto [his] voice." (Moses 4:4.) And so this personage who was an angel of God and in authority, even in the presence of God, was removed from the presence of God and his Son. (See D&C 76:25.) This caused great sadness in the heavens, "for the heavens wept over him—he was Lucifer, a son of the morning." (D&C 76:26.) Does this not place some responsibility on the followers of Christ to show concern for loved ones who have lost their way and "are shut out from the presence of God"? (Moses 6:49.) I know of no better way to do this than to show unconditional love and to help lost souls seek another path.

Satan does perform an important negative function. In 2 Nephi 2:11 we are told, "For it must needs be, that there is an opposition in all things." However, Peter warns, "Be sober, be vigilant; because our adversary the devil, as a roaring lion, walketh about, seeking who he may devour." (1 Peter 5:8.)

Let us not become so intense in our zeal to do good by winning arguments or by our pure intention in disputing doctrine that we go beyond good sense and manners, thereby promoting contention, or say or do imprudent things, invoke cynicism, or ridicule with flippancy. In this manner, our good motives become so misdirected that we lose friends and, even more serious, we come under the influence of the devil. I recently heard this truth: "Your criticism may be worse than the conduct you are trying to correct."

C. S. Lewis gives us a keen insight into devilish tactics. In a fictional letter, the master devil, Screwtape, instructs the apprentice devil Wormwood, who is in training to become a more experienced devil: "You will say that these are very small sins; and doubtless, like all young tempters, you are anxious to report spectacular wickedness. . . . It does not matter how small the sins are, provided that their cumulative effect is to edge the man away from the Light and out into the Nothing. . . . Indeed, the safest road to Hell is the gradual one—the gentle slope, soft underfoot, without sudden turnings, without milestones, without signposts." (*The Screwtape Letters*, New York: Macmillan, 1962, p. 56.)

Lewis also wrote: "A silly idea is current that good people do not know what temptation means. This is an obvious lie. Only those who try to resist temptation know how strong it is. . . . You find out the strength of a wind by trying to walk against it, not by lying down." (*Mere Christianity*, New York: Macmillan, 1960, p. 124.)

The Prophet Joseph Smith related from experience, "The nearer a person approaches the Lord, a greater power will be manifested by the adversary to prevent the accomplishment of His purpose." (Quoted in Orson F. Whitney, *Life of Heber C. Kimball*, p. 132.)

However, we need not become paralyzed with fear of Satan's power. He can have no power over us unless we permit it. He is really a coward, and if we stand firm, he will retreat. The Apostle James counseled: "Submit yourselves

therefore to God. Resist the devil, and he will flee from you."
(James 4:7.) He cannot know our thoughts unless we speak
them.

We have heard comedians and others justify or explain
their misdeeds by saying, "The devil made me do it." I do
not really think the devil can make us do anything. Certainly
he can tempt and he can deceive, but he has no authority
over us that we do not give him.

The power to resist Satan may be stronger than we realize.
The Prophet Joseph Smith taught: "All beings who have bodies have power over those who have not. The devil has no
power over us only as we permit him. The moment we revolt
at anything which comes from God, the devil takes power."
(*Teachings of the Prophet Joseph Smith*, p. 181.) He also stated,
"Wicked spirits have their bounds, limits, and laws by which
they are governed." (*History of the Church* 4:576.)

So Satan and his angels are not all-powerful. One of his
approaches is to persuade a person who has transgressed that
there is no hope for forgiveness. But there is always hope.
Most sins, no matter how grievous, may be repented of if the
desire is sincere enough.

Satan has had great success with the gullible generation.
As a consequence, he and his angels have victimized literally
hosts of people. There is, however, an ample shield against
their power. This protection lies in the spirit of discernment
through the gift of the Holy Ghost. This gift comes unde-
viatingly by personal revelation to those who strive to obey
the commandments of the Lord and follow the counsel of the
living prophets. Personal revelation will surely come to all
whose eyes are single to the glory of God, for it is promised
that their bodies will be "filled with light, and there shall be
no darkness" in them. (D&C 88:67.) Satan's efforts can be
thwarted by all who come unto Christ by obedience to the

covenants and ordinances of the gospel. Humble followers of the divine Master need not be deceived by the devil if they are honest and true to their fellow beings, go to the house of the Lord, receive the sacrament worthily, observe the Sabbath day, pay their tithes and offerings, offer contrite prayers, engage in the Lord's work, and follow those who preside over them.

I testify that there are forces that will save us from the ever-increasing lying, disorder, violence, chaos, destruction, misery, and deceit that are upon the earth. Those saving forces are the everlasting principles, covenants, and ordinances of the eternal gospel of the Lord Jesus Christ. These same principles, covenants, and ordinances are coupled with the rights and powers of the priesthood of Almighty God. Members of the Church are the possessors and custodians of these commanding powers, which can and do roll back much of the power of Satan on the earth. We believe that we hold these mighty forces in trust for all who have died, for all who are now living, and for all who are yet unborn.

I pray that, through the spreading of righteousness, the evil hands of the destroyer might be stayed and that he may not be permitted to curse the whole world. I also pray that God will overlook our weaknesses, our frailties, and our many shortcomings and generously forgive us of our misdeeds, and that He will bring solace to the suffering, comfort to those who grieve, and peace to the brokenhearted.

Chapter 15

LIGHT AND
KNOWLEDGE
FROM ABOVE

Constant communication with God, through the process known as divine revelation, is basic to our belief. President Wilford Woodruff declared: "Whenever the Lord had a people on the earth that He acknowledged as such, that people were led by revelation." (*Journal of Discourses* 24:240.) The inspiration of God is available to all who worthily seek the guidance of the Holy Spirit. This is particularly true of those who have received the gift of the Holy Ghost. I wish to discuss here, however, God's communications to all of his children through prophets, as distinguished from personal revelation received by individual members of the Church and others. The prophets, seers, and revelators have had and still have the responsibility and privilege of receiving and declaring the word of God for the world. Individual members, parents, and leaders have the right to receive revelation for their own responsibility but have no duty or right to declare the word of God beyond the limits of their own responsibility.

The ninth article of faith states: "We believe all that God has revealed, all that He does now reveal, and we believe that He will yet reveal many great and important things pertaining to the Kingdom of God."

Through the ages, God's messages to his children generally have been revealed through prophets. Amos tells us, "Surely the Lord God will do nothing, but he revealeth his secret unto his servants the prophets." (Amos 3:7.) These are the prophetic oracles who have tuned in over the centuries to the "celestial transmitting station," with a responsibility to relay the Lord's word to others. The principal qualifications of a prophet in any age are not wealth, title, position, physical stature, scholarship, or intellectual attainment. The two qualifications of a prophet are, first, that he must be called as such by God, by prophecy, and ordained by one known to have legal and spiritual authority, and, second, he must receive and declare revelation from God. (See D&C 42:11.) No man knows the ways of God except they be revealed unto him. (See Jacob 4:8.)

Over the centuries revelation from prophets has come incrementally. The Lord declared: "For [God] will give unto the faithful line upon line, precept upon precept; and I [the Lord] will try you and prove you herewith." (D&C 98:12.)

Revelations have come by various means, including by guidance of the Holy Ghost (which is perhaps most common), by the spoken word, and by visits from holy messengers.

The ninth article of faith says that we believe "all that [God] does now reveal." For some strange reason it seems easier for many to believe the words of dead prophets rather than those of living prophets. The greatest revelator in our time has been Joseph Smith. In the difficult period between 1823 and 1843, just twenty years, 134 revelations were received, printed, and made public.

Each of the apostles called since then has been sustained as a prophet, seer, and revelator, but those succeeding Joseph as president of the Church have been those apostles in whom *all* of the keys of Christ's earthly kingdom have been active and functioning.

I do not believe members of the Church can be in full harmony with the Savior without sustaining his living prophet on the earth, the president of the Church. If we do not sustain the living prophet, whoever he may be, we die spiritually. Ironically, some have died spiritually by exclusively following prophets who have long been dead. Others equivocate in their support of living prophets, trying to lift themselves up by putting down the living prophets, however subtly.

In our lifetime we have been favored with ongoing communication from the heavens, which have been open to the prophets of our time. Major divine pronouncements have included what we now know as section 138 of the Doctrine and Covenants, given in 1918. Surely one of the greatest divine disclosures came in 1978 when the blessings of the priesthood and temple became available to all worthy male members. Line upon line and precept upon precept, new knowledge and direction have been given to the Church.

Thus, by revelation in our day the Seventies have been given an expanded role as members of area presidencies and in general Church administration, helping the First Presidency and the Twelve "in building up the church and regulating all the affairs of the same in all nations." (D&C 107:34.) Many other divine instructions have also been received. Much revelation received, in this time as well as anciently, has been doctrinal. Some of it has been operational and tactical. Much of it is not spectacular. President John Taylor reminds us: "Adam's revelation did not instruct Noah to build his ark; nor did Noah's revelation tell Lot to forsake Sodom; nor did either of these speak of the departure of the children of Israel from Egypt. These all had revelations for themselves." (*Millennial Star*, November 1, 1847, p. 323.)

In our time God has revealed how to administer the

111

Church with a membership of millions differently than when there were just six members. These differences include the use of modern technology, such as films, computers, and satellite broadcasts, to teach and communicate new ways to conduct missionary work in various nations; the location and building of temples; and many others.

This process of continuous revelation comes to the Church frequently. President Wilford Woodruff stated, "This power is in the bosom of Almighty God, and he imparts it to his servants the prophets as they stand in need of it day by day to build up Zion." (*Journal of Discourses* 14:33.) This is necessary for the Church to fulfill its mission. Without it, we would fail.

An encouraging portion of the ninth article of faith is its conclusion, "We believe that He will yet reveal many great and important things pertaining to the Kingdom of God." Elder Boyd K. Packer has written: "Revelation is a continuous principle in the Church. In one sense the Church is still being organized. As light and knowledge are given, as prophecies are fulfilled and more intelligence is received, another step forward can be taken." (*The Holy Temple,* Salt Lake City: Bookcraft, 1980, p. 137.)

The Church constantly needs the guidance of its head, the Lord and Savior, Jesus Christ. This was well taught by President George Q. Cannon: "We have the Bible, the Book of Mormon and the Book of Doctrine and Covenants; but all these books, without the living oracles and a constant stream of revelation from the Lord, would not lead any people into the Celestial Kingdom. . . . This may seem a strange declaration to make, but strange as it may sound, it is nevertheless true.

"Of course, these records are all of infinite value. They cannot be too highly prized, nor can they be too closely studied. But in and of themselves, with all the light that they give, they are insufficient to guide the children of men and to lead them into the presence of God. To be thus led requires a living Priesthood and constant revelation from God to the people according to the circumstances in which they may be placed." (*Gospel Truth*, Classics in Mormon Literature Series, 2 vols. in one, Salt Lake City: Deseret Book, 1987, p. 252.)

When will this promised revelation come? Only God knows when. It will come as needed. To whom will it come? To obtain the answer to this, we must go back to the words of Amos: "Surely the Lord God will do nothing, but he revealeth his secret unto his servants the prophets." (Amos 3:7.) Continuous revelation will not and cannot be forced by outside pressure from people and events. It is not the so-called "revelation of social progress." It does not originate with the prophets; it comes from God. The Church is governed by the prophet under the guidance and direction of God.

Parley P. Pratt disclosed: "The legislative, judicial, and executive power is vested in [the Lord]. He reveals the laws, and he elects, chooses, or appoints the officers; and holds the right to reprove, correct, or even to remove them at pleasure. Hence the necessity of a constant intercourse by direct revelation between him and his church." (*Millennial Star*, March 1845, p. 150.)

We have been promised that the president of the Church will receive guidance for all of us as the revelator for the Church. Our safety lies in paying heed to what he says and following his counsel.

The doctrine of the Church was stated by Elder Stephen L Richards: "They [the Presidency] are the supreme court here on earth in the interpretation of God's law. In the exercise of their functions and delegated powers they are controlled

113

by a constitution, a part of which is written and a part of which is not. The written part consists in authenticated scripture, ancient and modern, and in the recorded utterances of our latter-day prophets. The unwritten part is the spirit of revelation and divine inspiration which are appertinent to their calling. In formulating their interpretations and decisions they always confer with the Council of the Twelve Apostles who by revelation are appointed to assist and act with them in the government of the Church. When, therefore, a judgment is reached and proclaimed by these officers it becomes binding upon all members of the Church, individual views to the contrary notwithstanding. God's Kingdom is a kingdom of law and order." (Conference Report, October 1938, pp. 115–16.)

How can we be sure that, as promised, the prophets, seers, and revelators will never lead this people astray? One answer is contained in the grand principle found in the Doctrine and Covenants: "And every decision made by either of these quorums [the First Presidency and the Quorum of the Twelve Apostles] must be by the unanimous voice of the same." (D&C 107:27.) This requirement of unanimity provides a check on bias and personal idiosyncrasies. It ensures that God rules through the Spirit, not man through majority or compromise. It ensures that the best wisdom and experience is focused on an issue before the deep, unassailable impressions of revealed direction are received. It guards against the foibles of man.

The responsibility for determining the divine validity of what one of the oracles of God states does not rest solely upon him. President J. Reuben Clark stated, "We can tell when the speakers are 'moved upon by the Holy Ghost' only when we, ourselves, are 'moved upon by the Holy Ghost.' " (David H. Yarn, Jr., ed., *J. Reuben Clark: Selected Papers on*

Religion, Education, and Youth, Provo: Brigham Young University Press, 1984, pp. 95–96.)

This is in harmony with the counsel of Brigham Young: "I am more afraid that this people have so much confidence in their leaders that they will not inquire for themselves of God whether they are led by Him. I am fearful they settle down in a state of blind self-security, trusting their eternal destiny in the hands of their leaders with a reckless confidence that in itself would thwart the purposes of God in their salvation, and weaken that influence they could give to their leaders, did they know for themselves, by the revelations of Jesus, that they are led in the right way. Let every man and woman know, by the whispering of the Spirit of God to themselves, whether their leaders are walking in the path the Lord dictates, or not." *(Journal of Discourses* 9:150.)

Revelation was required to establish the Church. Revelation has brought it from it from humble beginnings to its present course. Revelation has come like flowing, living water. Continuing revelation will lead it forward to the windup scene. But as President Clark told us, we do not need more or different prophets. We need more people with "a listening ear." (Conference Report, October 1948, p. 82.)

We make no claim of infallibility or perfection in the prophets, seers, and revelators. Yet I humbly state that I have sat in the company of these men, and I believe their greatest desire is to know and do the will of our Heavenly Father. Those who sit in the highest councils of the Church and have participated as inspiration has come and decisions have been reached know that this light and truth is beyond human intelligence and reasoning. These deep, divine impressions have come as the dews from heaven and settled upon them individually and collectively. So inspired, we can go forward in complete unity and accord.

Chapter 16

THE HOLY GHOST:
A SURE COMFORTER

A profoundly moving event occurred centuries ago when the Savior led his beloved disciples into the favored Garden of Gethsemane for the last time. Jesus was mindful of the great ordeal ahead of him. He agonized, "My soul is exceeding sorrowful unto death: tarry ye here, and watch." He was ready for the unspeakable agony. Said he, "The spirit truly is ready, but the flesh is weak." (Mark 14:34, 38.)

The eleven apostles no doubt sensed—but could not understand—that some portentous event would happen. Jesus had spoken of leaving them. They knew that the Master whom they loved and depended upon was going somewhere, but where, they did not know. They had heard him say, "I will not leave you comfortless. . . . But the Comforter, which is the Holy Ghost, whom the Father will send in my name, he shall teach you all things, and bring all things to your remembrance, whatsoever I have said unto you." (John 14:18, 26.)

Elder LeGrand Richards stated, "It must . . . be understood that the Holy Ghost is the medium through whom God and his Son, Jesus Christ, communicate with men upon the earth." (*A Marvelous Work and a Wonder*, rev. ed., Salt Lake

City: Deseret Book, 1976, p. 119.) All people are enlightened by the Spirit of God, or Light of Christ, which is sometimes called conscience. Job stated, "There is a spirit in man: and the inspiration of the Almighty giveth them understanding." (Job 32:8.) This is the Spirit of God emanating from Deity. This power is the means by which, as President Joseph F. Smith stated, "every man is enlightened, the wicked as well as the good, the intelligent and the ignorant, the high and the low, each in accordance with his capacity to receive the light." (*Gospel Doctrine*, Salt Lake City: Deseret Book, 1939, p. 62; see also D&C 88:3–13.)

The gift of the Holy Ghost, in distinction from the Spirit of God, does not come to all persons. The ministrations of the Holy Ghost are, however, limited unless one receives the gift of the Holy Ghost. The Prophet Joseph Smith taught that "there is a difference between the Holy Ghost and the gift of the Holy Ghost." (*Teachings of the Prophet Joseph Smith*, p. 199.) Many outside the Church have received revelation from the Holy Ghost, convincing them of the truth of the gospel. Cornelius, as well as many in attendance on the day of Pentecost, received the Holy Ghost before baptism. (See Acts 2:1–12; 10:30–44.) It is through this power that seekers after truth acquire a testimony of the Book of Mormon and the principles of the gospel.

The gift of the Holy Ghost comes after one repents and becomes worthy. It is received after baptism by the laying on of hands by those who have authority. On the day of Pentecost, Peter instructed those who had previously been touched spiritually by the Holy Ghost, "Repent, and be baptized every one of you for the remission of sins, and ye shall receive the gift of the Holy Ghost." (Acts 2:38.) Those possessing the gift of the Holy Ghost can come to a greater light and testimony. The Holy Ghost bears witness of the truth

117

and impresses upon the soul the reality of God the Father and his Son, Jesus Christ, so deeply that no earthly power or authority can separate him from that knowledge. (See 2 Nephi 31:18.)

The Book of Mormon, the Bible, and other scriptures, along with the guidance of modern prophets, provide true standards of conduct. In addition, the gift of the Holy Ghost is available as a sure guide, as the voice of conscience, and as a moral compass. This guiding compass is personal to each of us. It is unerring. It is unfailing. However, we must listen to it in order to steer clear of the shoals that can cause our lives to sink into unhappiness and self-doubt.

We need a sure compass because many of the standards, values, vows, and obligations that have helped us preserve our spirituality, our honor, our integrity, our worth, and our decency have little by little been assaulted and discarded. I speak, among other values, of the standards of chastity, parental respect, fidelity in marriage, and obedience to God's laws — such as Sabbath observance — which have been weakened, if not destroyed. Society has been misled.

Thomas R. Rowan, in an address to the National Press Club, commented on the lowering of television standards. He said, "Author and commentator Malcolm Muggeridge once told a story about some frogs who were killed without resistance by being boiled alive in the cauldron of water. Why didn't they resist? Because when they were put in the cauldron, the water was tepid. Then the temperature was raised ever so slightly, and the water was warm, then a tiny bit warmer, then a bit warmer still, and on and on and on. The change was so gradual, almost imperceptible, that the frogs accommodated themselves to their new environment — until it was too late. The point that Mr. Muggeridge was making was not about frogs but about us and how we tend to accept evil as long as it is not a shock that is thrust on us abruptly. We are inclined to accept something morally wrong if it is only a shade more wrong than something we are already accepting."

This gradual process was foretold by ancient prophets. Nephi tells us that Satan would stir up the hearts of the children of men "to anger against that which is good. And others will he pacify, and lull them away into carnal security, that they will say: All is well in Zion; yea, Zion prospereth, all is well—and thus the devil cheateth their souls, and leadeth them away carefully down to hell." (2 Nephi 28:20–21.)

I have always been fascinated that people are led *carefully* down to hell.

Alexander Pope expressed a similar thought concerning the acceptance of evil:

> Vice is a monster of so frightful mien
> As to be hated needs but to be seen;
> Yet seen too often, familiar with her face,
> We first endure, then pity, then embrace.

The gift of the Holy Ghost will prompt us to resist temptation by reminding us of the gospel law in the very moment of temptation. Said Elder B. H. Roberts, "By having the Holy Spirit as one's prompter in the moments of temptation, . . . this law of the Gospel . . . may be complied with." (*The Gospel: An Exposition of Its First Principles and Man's Relationship to Deity*, Salt Lake City: Deseret Book, 1965, pp. 191–92.)

I wish to alert young people of this special, transcendent gift of the Holy Ghost, which is available to all. This Comforter is a personage of spirit and a member of the Godhead. The Doctrine and Covenants explains why the Holy Ghost is a personage of spirit: "The Father has a body of flesh and bones as tangible as man's; the Son also; but the Holy Ghost has

119

not a body of flesh and bones, but is a personage of Spirit. Were it not so, the Holy Ghost could not dwell in us." (D&C 130:22.)

The gift of the Holy Ghost entitles a person who is desirous and worthy to enjoy "the power and light of truth of the Holy Ghost." (Joseph F. Smith, *Gospel Doctrine*, p. 61.)

The comforting Spirit of the Holy Ghost can abide with us twenty-four hours a day: when we work, when we play, when we rest. Its strengthening influence can be with us year in and year out. That sustaining influence can be with us in joy and sorrow, when we rejoice as well as when we grieve.

I believe the Spirit of the Holy Ghost is the greatest guarantor of inward peace in our unstable world. It can be more mind-expanding and make us have a better sense of well-being than any chemical or other earthly substance. It will calm nerves; it will breathe peace to our souls. This Comforter can be with us as we seek to improve. It can function as a source of revelation to warn us of impending danger and also help keep us from making mistakes. It can enhance our natural senses so that we can see more clearly, hear more keenly, and remember what we should remember. It is a way of maximizing our happiness.

The Spirit—the Holy Ghost—will help us work out our insecurities. For instance, it can help us learn to forgive. There comes a time when people must move on, seeking greater things rather than being consumed by the memory of some hurt or injustice. Dwelling constantly on past injuries is, by its nature, limiting to the Spirit. It does not promote peace.

The Holy Ghost will also help us solve crises of faith. The Spirit of the Holy Ghost can be a confirming witness, testifying of heavenly things. Through that Spirit, a strong knowledge distills in one's mind, and one feels all doubt or questions disappear.

The Apostle Paul said, "For the kingdom of God is not meat and drink; but righteousness, and peace, and joy in the Holy Ghost." (Romans 14:17.) He also said that true Saints are the "temple of the Holy Ghost." (1 Corinthians 6:19.) I wish to say a word about the Holy Spirit of Promise, which is the sealing and ratifying power of the Holy Ghost. To have a covenant or ordinance sealed by the Holy Spirit of Promise is a compact through which the inherent blessings will be obtained, if those seeking the blessing are true and faithful. (See D&C 76:50–54.)

For example, when the covenant of marriage for time and eternity, the culminating gospel ordinance, is sealed by the Holy Spirit of Promise, it can literally open the windows of heaven for great blessings to flow to a married couple who seek for those blessings. Such marriages become rich, whole, and sacred. Though each party to the marriage can maintain his or her separate identity, yet together in their covenants they can be like two vines wound inseparably around each other. Each thinks of his or her companion before thinking of self.

One of the great blessings available through the Holy Spirit of Promise is that all of our covenants, vows, oaths, and performances, which we receive through the ordinances and blessings of the gospel, are not only confirmed but may be sealed by the Holy Spirit of Promise. However, that sealing may be broken by unrighteousness. It is also important to remember that if a person undertakes to receive the sealing blessing by deceit, "then the blessing is not sealed, notwithstanding the integrity and authority of the person officiating." (Joseph Fielding Smith, *Doctrines of Salvation*, Bookcraft, 1955, 2:98–99.) To have a covenant or ordinance sealed by the Holy Spirit of Promise means that the compact is binding on earth and in heaven.

It is always gratifying to hear of prayers being answered and miracles occurring in the lives of those who need them. But what of those noble and faithful souls who receive no miracles, whose prayers are not answered in the way they wish? What is their solace? Where will their comfort come from? Said the Savior of the world, "I will not leave you comfortless: I will come to you. . . . But the Comforter, which is the Holy Ghost, . . . the Father will send in my name." (John 14:18, 26.)

In simple terms, the gift of the Holy Ghost is an enhanced spiritual power permitting those entitled to receive it to receive a greater knowledge and enjoyment of the influence of Deity.

In February 1847, the Prophet Joseph appeared to Brigham Young in a dream or vision. Brigham pleaded to be reunited with the Prophet and asked if he had a message for the Brethren. The Prophet said: "Tell the people to be humble and faithful, and to be sure to keep the Spirit of the Lord and it will lead them right. Be careful and not turn away the still small voice; it will teach them what to do and where to go; it will yield the fruits of the kingdom. Tell the Brethren to keep their hearts open to conviction, so that when the Holy Ghost comes to them, their hearts will be ready to receive it."

The Prophet further directed Brigham, "They can tell the Spirit of the Lord from all other spirits; it will whisper peace and joy to their souls; it will take malice, hatred, strife and all evil from their hearts; and their whole desire will be to do good, bring forth righteousness and build up the kingdom of God." (*Manuscript History of Brigham Young: 1846–47,* Historical Department, The Church of Jesus Christ of Latter-day Saints, pp. 528–31.)

If in this life we cannot live in the presence of the Savior as did Simon Peter, James, John, Mary, Martha, and others, then the gift of the Holy Ghost can be our Comforter and sure compass.

I testify that as we mature spiritually under the guidance of the Holy Ghost, our sense of personal worth, of belonging, and of identity increases. I further testify that I would rather have every person enjoy the Spirit of the Holy Ghost than any other association, for they will be led by that Spirit to light and truth and pure intelligence, which can carry them back into the presence of God.

Chapter 17

COMMUNION WITH THE HOLY SPIRIT

At the Samoa area conference in 1976, President Spencer W. Kimball said: "Often when we have press conferences, the press asks us this question: "What is the greatest problem that your . . . Church has today?" We answer that it is rapid growth. It is very difficult to keep up with the growth of the Church in many lands."

It has been some 160 years since The Church of Jesus Christ of Latter-day Saints was organized. Why does the Church continue to flourish and grow so dramatically? What distinguishes it from all other churches? We believe that we can answer questions more correctly than anyone else. Several characteristics are peculiar to our faith. These include the organization itself, with prophets and apostles, who Paul said are the foundation of the Church (see Ephesians 2:20); the First Quorum of the Seventy; lay priesthood leadership; the missionary system; the welfare program; temples; the genealogical effort, and many other distinguishing features.

There is, however, another reason for our growth, one that transcends all others. Of an interview in 1839 between the Prophet Joseph Smith and Martin Van Buren, who was then president of the United States, the following was recorded: "In our interview with the President, he interrogated us wherein we differed in our religion from the other religions of the day. Brother Joseph said we differed in mode of baptism, and the gift of the Holy Ghost by the laying on of hands. We considered that all other considerations were contained in the gift of the Holy Ghost." (*History of the Church* 4:42.)

One of the reasons the Prophet's response was so inspired is that the right to enjoy the marvelous gifts of the Holy Ghost is conferred upon every member of the Church soon after baptism. This is in fulfillment of the promise of the Savior: "And I will pray the Father, and he shall give you another Comforter, that he may abide with you for ever." (John 14:16.)

This powerful gift entitles the leaders and all worthy members of the Church to enjoy the gifts and companionship of the Holy Ghost, a member of the Godhead whose function is to inspire, reveal, and teach all things. The result of this endowment is that since the Church was organized, the leadership and members have enjoyed, and now enjoy, continuous revelation and inspiration directing them in what is right and good. Inspiration and revelation are so common, so widespread, so universal among the leaders and the members that there is a strong spiritual base underlying what is done. This can be found in the gatherings of the Church, both large and small.

Why does the Church grow and flourish? It does so because of divine direction to the leaders and members. This began in our day when God the Father and Jesus Christ appeared to Joseph Smith early in the spring of 1820. However, we claim that God's inspiration is not limited to the Latter-day Saints. The First Presidency has stated: "The great religious leaders of the world such as Mohammed, Confucius, and the Reformers, as well as philosophers including Socrates, Plato, and others, received a portion of God's light. Moral truths were given to them by God to enlighten whole

125

nations and to bring a higher level of understanding to individuals. . . . We believe that God has given and will give to all peoples sufficient knowledge to help them on their way to eternal salvation." (*Statement of the First Presidency Regarding God's Love for All Mankind*, February 15, 1978.)

We declare in all solemnity, however, that we know salvation in the world to come is dependent upon accepting the gospel of Jesus Christ as taught in The Church of Jesus Christ of Latter-day Saints. One factor in salvation is personal revelation. Joseph Smith said: "No man can receive the Holy Ghost without receiving revelations. The Holy Ghost is a revelator." (*History of the Church* 6:58.)

Latter-day Saints, having received the gift of the Holy Ghost by the laying on of hands, are entitled to personal inspiration in the small events of life as well as when they are confronted with the giant Goliaths of life.

David, the youngest son of Jesse, a mere shepherd boy, volunteered to fight the giant Goliath. David and all of the army of Israel were insulted by the humiliating taunts of this formidable giant, but David knew that inspiration had brought him to save Israel. King Saul was so impressed with the faith and determination of this young boy that he appointed him to fight Goliath. Goliath made sport of David's youth and lack of armament. David responded that he came in the name of the Lord of Hosts, the God of the armies of Israel, and that the whole assembly would learn that the Lord does not save by the sword and the spear, "for the battle is the Lord's." (1 Samuel 17:47.) Then David threw a rock from his sling with such force and accuracy that the stone sank deep into the forehead of Goliath. Goliath fell to the earth a dying man, and the Philistines fled in fear.

What has happened to David's living God? It is the greatest insult to reason to suggest that God, who spoke so freely to the prophets of the Old Testament, now stands mute, uncommunicative, and silent.

We may well ask, Does God love us less than those led by the ancient prophets? Do we need his guidance and instruction less? Reason suggests that this cannot be. Does he not care? Has he lost his voice? Has he gone on a permanent vacation? Does he sleep? The unreasonableness of each of these proposals is self-evident.

When the Savior taught in the synagogue at Capernaum, he proclaimed his divinity in no uncertain terms. The apostle John states: "From that time many of his disciples went back, and walked no more with him. Then said Jesus unto the twelve, Will ye also go away? Then Simon Peter answered him, Lord, to whom shall we go? thou hast the words of eternal life. And we believe and are sure that thou art that Christ, the Son of the living God." (John 6:66–69.)

We acknowledge and testify that the same witness of Christ's divinity as received by Peter is also our sacred knowledge.

Personal revelation comes as a testimony of truth and as guidance in spiritual and temporal matters. Latter-day Saints know that the promptings of the Spirit may be received upon all facets of life, including daily, ongoing decisions. Without seeking the inspiration of the Almighty God, how could anyone think of making an important decision such as "Who is to be my companion?" "What is my work to be?" "Where will I live?" "How will I live?"

Many faithful Latter-day Saints have been warned by the Spirit when they were faced with injury or possible death. Among these was President Wilford Woodruff, who said:

"When I got back to Winter Quarters from the pioneer journey [1847], President Young said to me, 'Brother Woodruff, I want you to take your wife and children and go to

Boston and stay there until you can gather every Saint of God in New England and Canada and send them up to Zion.' I did as he told me. It took me two years to gather up everybody, and I brought up the rear with a company (there were about one hundred of them). We arrived at Pittsburgh one day at sundown. We did not want to stay there, so I went to the first steamboat that was going to leave. I saw the captain and engaged passage for us on that steamer. I had only just done so when the spirit said to me, and that, too, very strongly, 'Don't go aboard that steamer, nor your company.' Of course, I went and spoke to the captain, and told him I had made up my mind to wait.

"Well, that ship started, and had only got five miles down the river when it took fire, and three hundred persons were burned to death or drowned. If I had not obeyed that spirit, and had gone on that steamer with the rest of the company, you can see what the result would have been." (*Discourses of Wilford Woodruff,* Salt Lake City: Bookcraft, 1946, pp. 294–95.)

Some guidelines and rules are necessary if one is to be the recipient of revelation and inspiration; they include (1) to try honestly and sincerely to keep God's commandments, (2) to be spiritually attuned as a receiver of a divine message, (3) to ask in humble, fervent prayer, and (4) to seek with unwavering faith.

I testify that inspiration can be the spring of every person's hope, guidance, and strength. It is one of the magnified treasures of life. It involves coming to the infinite knowledge of God.

How do revelation and inspiration operate? Each person has a built-in "receiving set" which, when fine-tuned, can be a receiver of divine communication. Said Job, "There is a spirit in man: and . . . the Almighty giveth them understanding." (Job 32:8.) It is possible, like Nephi, to be led completely by the Spirit, "not knowing beforehand" what should be done. (See 1 Nephi 4:6.)

How is inspiration received? Enos stated, "While I was thus struggling in the spirit, behold, the voice of the Lord came into my mind." (Enos 1:10.) One does not necessarily hear an audible voice. The spirit of revelation comes by divine confirmation. "I will tell you in your mind and in your heart, by the Holy Ghost, which shall come upon you and which shall dwell in your heart," says the Lord. (D&C 8:2.)

How was the voice of the Lord heard by Elijah the Tishbite? It was not the "strong wind [which] rent the mountains, and brake in pieces the rock," nor "after the wind an earthquake," nor "after the earthquake a fire." It was "a still small voice." (See 1 Kings 19:11–12.)

The inner voice of the Spirit has the capacity to whisper through and pierce all things. (See D&C 85:6.) Helaman says, "It was not a voice of thunder, neither was it a voice of great tumultuous noise, but behold, it was a still voice of perfect mildness, as if it had been a whisper, and it did pierce even to the very soul." (Helaman 5:30.)

Thus the Lord, by revelation, brings inspiration into one's mind as though a voice were speaking. As a member of the Council of the Twelve Apostles, Harold B. Lee gave this testimony: "I have a believing heart because of a simple testimony that came when I was a child, I think maybe I was around ten—maybe eleven—years of age. I was with my father out on a farm away from our home, trying to spend the day busying myself until father was ready to go home.

"Over the fence from our place were some tumbledown sheds which had attracted a curious boy, adventurous as I was. I started to climb through the fence and I heard a voice as clearly as you are hearing mine—'Don't go over there!' calling me by name. I turned to look at father to see if he were talking to me, but he was way up at the other end of the field. There was no person in sight. I realized then, as a child, that there were persons beyond my sight and I had heard a voice. And when I hear and read these stories of the Prophet Joseph Smith, I, too, know what it means to hear a voice because I've heard from an unseen speaker." (*Brigham Young University Speeches of the Year*, Provo: October 15, 1952, p. 6.)

Although every faithful member of the Church is entitled to receive personal revelation, there is only one man upon the earth who receives revelation for the Church. President Wilford Woodruff said, "The Church of God could not live twenty-four hours without revelation." (*Discourses of Wilford Woodruff*, p. 61.)

Author Roy W. Doxey reminds us: "Every day men and women come, by revelation, to understand the basic truth that God has restored his Gospel and Church.

"Every day leaders of the Church are led by revelation to conduct the affairs of the Church, general and local, throughout the world.

"Every day Latter-day Saint missionaries are impressed by the spirit of revelation to bear witness, to know what to say, to know what to do, and to teach by the spirit of revelation.

"Every day the mind and will of the Lord as revealed in the standard works of the Church are illuminated in the minds of the Latter-day Saints by the spirit of revelation.

"Every day faith is increased in the hearts of the faithful by evidences of revelation in their lives—in decisions regarding marriage, vocations, home concerns, business ventures, lesson preparations, danger signals—in fact, in all facets of life.

"Every Latter-day Saint may know by the spirit of revelation that President Joseph Fielding Smith spoke the truth when he said: 'The Lord not only blesses the men who stand at the head and hold the keys of the kingdom, but *he also blesses every faithful individual with the spirit of inspiration.'* (*Doctrines of Salvation* 1:281–82.)" (*Walk with the Lord,* Salt Lake City: Deseret Book, 1973, pp. 173–74.)

On June 1, 1978, one of the greatest revelations ever received in the history of the world came to mankind. It was revealed that all worthy brethren in the Church, regardless of color or race, could receive the priesthood.

Who is the prophet of the world today? I testify that the prophet upon the face of the earth today is the man who serves as the president of the Church. The Church of Jesus Christ of Latter-day Saints is God's Church upon the earth, and salvation in God's presence requires acceptance of the fullness of the gospel of Jesus Christ as taught in his church.

Why has the Church grown so dramatically over more than a century and a half? Why does it continue to grow at an ever-increasing pace? It does so in large measure because of divine revelation and inspiration.

I pray that we may so live as to enjoy the companionship of the Holy Ghost, for the Holy Ghost, under the direction of Almighty God, has led this people and their leaders from the Church's humble beginnings to the great spiritual force it is today.

Chapter 18

THE SUPERNAL GIFT
OF THE ATONEMENT

Through the atonement and those singular events surrounding it, all of the terrible individual and collective sins of mankind were taken upon the Lord's shoulders. The marvelous result of this great suffering was that he was able to redeem from physical death the believers and the obedient as well as the unbelieving and disobedient. (D&C 46:13–14; Acts 24:15; 1 Corinthians 15:22.) Every person ever born or yet to be born is the beneficiary of both the mediation and the atonement of the Savior. (Alma 11:42.)

The act of the atonement is, in its simplest terms, a reconciliation of man with his God. The word *atonement* means to be at one. According to Elder James E. Talmage, "It is literally *at-one-ment.*" (*Articles of Faith*, p. 75.) Because of their transgression, Adam and Eve, having chosen to leave their state of innocence (2 Nephi 2:23–25), were banished from the presence of God. This is referred to in Christendom as the Fall, or Adam's transgression. It is a spiritual death because Adam and Eve were separated from the presence of God and given agency "to act for themselves and not to be acted upon." (2 Nephi 2:26.) They were also given the power of procreation, so that they could keep the commandment to "multiply, and replenish the earth" and have joy in their posterity. (Genesis 1:28.)

132

All of their posterity were likewise banished from the presence of God. However, Adam and Eve's descendants were innocent of the original sin because they had no part in it. It was therefore unfair for all of humanity to suffer eternally for the transgressions of our first parents, Adam and Eve. It became necessary for this injustice to be settled; hence the need for the atoning sacrifice of Jesus in his role as the Savior and Redeemer. Because of the transcendent act of the atonement, it is possible for every soul to obtain forgiveness of sins, to have them washed away and be forgotten. (2 Nephi 9:6–9; Talmage, *Articles of Faith,* p. 89.) This forgiveness comes about, however, on condition of repentance and personal righteousness.

There is a distinction between immortality, or eternal existence, and eternal life, which is to have a place in the presence of God. Through the grace of Jesus Christ, immortality comes to all persons, just or unjust, righteous or wicked. However, eternal life is "the greatest of all the gifts of God." We obtain this great gift, according to the Lord, if we keep his commandments and "endure to the end." If we so endure, the promise is, "you shall have eternal life." (D&C 14:7.)

President Joseph Fielding Smith explains, "This distinction between *eternal life,* as received by the faithful, and *immortality,* obtained by both the faithful and the unfaithful, is shown in the words of the Lord to Moses: 'For behold, this is my work and my glory—to bring to pass the immortality *and* eternal life of man.' The conjunction clearly separates the two thoughts. It explains that the Lord is giving to the vast majority of men, those who will not be obedient, the blessing of immortality; and to those who will serve him, the blessing of eternal life." (*The Way to Perfection,* Salt Lake City: The Genealogical Society of Utah, 1946, p. 329.)

It has been almost two thousand years since the wondrous

occasion when death was conquered. We still do not know how the Savior was able to take upon himself and bear our transgressions, our foolishness, our grief, our sorrows, and our burdens. It was indefinable and unfathomable. It was almost unbearable. The indescribable agony was so great in Gethsemane that "his sweat was as it were great drops of blood falling down to the ground." (Luke 22:44.) The haunting cry on the cross, in a loud voice in his native Aramaic—"Eloi, Eloi, lama sabachthani? which is, being interpreted, My God, my God, why hast thou forsaken me?" (Mark 15:34)—gives but a mere glimpse of his suffering and humiliation. One cannot help wondering how many of those drops of precious blood each of us may be responsible for.

Even though, as a man or a woman, we are born, live a brief moment, and then die, through the atonement of Jesus Christ we will all live after death. Through the divinity which is within us as a gift of the great Creator, we can come to complete fruition as heirs of God with eternal powers, dominions, and progression without end. Paul said the gift is a free gift. (Romans 5:15.) Through the mediation and the atonement we will be resurrected ourselves without going through any part of the atoning agony that the Son of God went through.

Jacob's teachings in the Book of Mormon further explain, "If the flesh should rise no more our spirits must become subject to the angels who fell from before the presence of the Eternal God, and became the devil, to rise no more." (2 Nephi 9:8.)

The testimonies of those faithful followers who saw, heard, and touched the resurrected Lord stand uncontroverted to this day. After the crucifixion, Mary Magdalene, Mary the mother of James, and Salome brought sweet spices to anoint his body. (Mark 16:1.)

But the devoted women were concerned as to who would roll away the great stone in front of the sepulchre. When they arrived, they found that the great stone had been rolled away. (Mark 16:3–4.) A great earthquake intervened, and an angel rolled back the stone from the door and sat upon it, causing the keepers to shake with fear and become as dead men. (Matthew 28:2–4.) The angel instructed the women to tell the disciples quickly of the Lord's resurrection, assuring them, "He goeth before you into Galilee; there shall ye see him." As they went to tell the disciples, "Jesus met them, saying, All hail. And they came and held him by the feet, and worshipped him." (Matthew 28:7, 9.)

During the forty days that the Savior spent with the apostles and others, they heard and saw many unspeakable things. This special ministry changed the apostles from an uncertain, confused, divided, and weak group into powerful witnesses of the Lord. Mark records that the Savior upbraided the eleven "because they believed not them which had seen him after he was risen." (Mark 16:14.)

Perhaps the apostles should not be unduly criticized for not believing that Jesus, having been crucified and buried in a tomb, had come back to earth as a glorified being. In all human experience, this had never happened before. This was completely unprecedented. This was a different experience from the raising of Jairus's daughter (Mark 5:22–24, 35–43), the young man of Nain (Luke 7:11–15), or Lazarus (John 11:1–44). They all died again. Jesus, however, became a resurrected being. He would never die again. So it was that to the apostles the story of Mary Magdalene and the other women who witnessed the resurrection "seemed to·them as idle tales, and they believed them not." (Luke 24:11.)

Said President David O. McKay of this experience: "The

world would never have been stirred by men with such wavering, doubting, despairing minds as the apostles possessed on the day of the crucifixion. What was it that suddenly changed these disciples to confident, fearless, heroic preachers of the gospel of Jesus Christ? It was the revelation that Christ had risen from the grave. His promises had been kept, his Messianic mission fulfilled. In the words of an eminent writer, 'The final and absolute seal of genuineness has been put on all his claims and the indelible stamp of divine authority upon all his teachings. The gloom of death had been banished by the glorious light of the presence of their Risen, Glorified Lord and Savior.' On the evidence of these unprejudiced, unexpectant, incredulous witnesses, faith in the resurrection has its impregnable foundation." (*Treasures of Life*, comp. Clare Middlemiss, Salt Lake City: Deseret Book, 1962, pp. 15–16.)

Like the apostles of old, this knowledge and belief should transform all of us to be confident, settled, unafraid, and at peace in our lives as followers of the divine Christ. It should help us carry all burdens, bear any sorrows, and fully savor all joys and happiness that can be found in this life. The disciples who walked with the Savior on the road to Emmaus said to one another, "Did not our heart burn within us, while he talked with us by the way, and while he opened to us the scriptures?" (Luke 24:32.) No wonder they entreated him, "Abide with us: for it is toward evening," and he "sat at meat with them." (Luke 24:29–30.) They sought to savor those precious moments and feelings.

The vacating of the tomb transcended all other events in the history of the world, for it attested that Jesus had not died, but that death itself had been overcome.

As I have traveled over much of the earth, I have been saddened over and over again by the legions of crippled, maimed, deformed, suffering, and diminished people almost

136

everywhere. What parent of a special child has not agonized over the future and well-being of that child? Through the individual resurrection of each of us, there is great hope for all.

Amulek, in the Book of Mormon, promises that following the temporal death, "the spirit and the body shall be reunited again in its perfect form; both limb and joint shall be restored to its proper frame, . . . and we shall be brought to stand before God, . . . and have a bright recollection of all our guilt." (Alma 11:43.)

The Prophet Joseph Smith stated, "I can taste the principles of eternal life, and so can you. . . . I know that when I tell you these words of eternal life . . . you taste them, and I know that you believe them." (*Teachings of the Prophet Joseph Smith,* p. 355.) So it is that the humblest and newest believer, the child, youth, or adult can come to have a personal conviction of the truth of eternal life.

John the Revelator "saw a new heaven and a new earth" and "heard a great voice out of heaven." (Revelation 21:1, 3.) "He that overcometh shall inherit all things; and I will be his God, and he shall be my son." (Revelation 21:7.) "And God shall wipe away all tears from their eyes; and there shall be no more death, neither sorrow, nor crying, neither shall there be any more pain: for the former things are passed away." (Revelation 21:4.)

It is not necessary for anyone to depend continually upon the testimony of another person regarding the mediation, atonement, and resurrection of Christ as our Redeemer and Savior. Each can savor the sweetness of the truths of the gospel by obedience to the principles, ordinances, and covenants. One can still go to the Garden of Gethsemane, but the Lord Jesus cannot be found there, nor is he in the Garden Tomb. He is not on the road to Emmaus, nor in Galilee, nor at Nazareth or Bethlehem. He must be found in one's heart. But he left us the great Comforter (John 14:16) and the everlasting power of the priesthood. Of this power, Jacob, the son of Lehi, testified, "We truly can command in the name of Jesus and the very trees obey us, or the mountains, or the waves of the sea." (Jacob 4:6.)

I testify that, through righteousness, this priesthood power and these supernal gifts of the atonement and the mediation can operate in our lives. Ultimately each of us must come to know these great spiritual truths by following the counsel of Jesus: "If any man will do his will, he shall know of the doctrine, whether it be of God, or whether I speak of myself." (John 7:17.)

In conclusion, I wish to humbly declare and affirm that Jesus is the Christ, our Redeemer, the Savior of the world. I do this with all the solemnity of my soul. This testimony has come to me not alone from a lifetime of study or from reason or logic, but more by personal revelation under the spirit of prophecy.

I pray that our Savior will heal our souls, dry our tears, and create in each of us a pure heart. I also pray that we may find shelter in the shadows of his outstretched arms and that he will be merciful and forgiving concerning our weaknesses. That he will be a father to the fatherless, and deliver to the needy according to their needs, and incline his ear to our cries, I humbly pray in the name of Jesus Christ. Amen.

SOURCES
OF CHAPTERS

The chapters in this book have been adapted from the following:
Chapter 1, "Reach Up for the Light": *Ensign,* May 1981, pp. 8–10.
Chapter 2, "Unwanted Messages and Hard Answers": *Ensign,* November 1982, pp. 8–10.
Chapter 3, "A Simple, Untroubled Faith": *Ensign,* March 1988, pp. 69–72.
Chapter 4, "Finding the Abundant Life": *Ensign,* November 1985, pp. 7–9.
Chapter 5, "Six Keys to Healthy Self-esteem": Education Week, Brigham Young University, August 1983.
Chapter 6, "The Need for Balance in Our Lives": Brigham Young University Devotional, March 1981.
Chapter 7, "Doing the Best Things in the Worst of Times": *Ensign,* August 1984, pp. 41–43.
Chapter 8, "Integrity, the Mother of Many Virtues": *Ensign,* May 1982, pp. 47–49.
Chapter 9, "Will I Be Happy?": *Ensign,* May 1987, pp. 80–82.
Chapter 10, "Caring for Ourselves and Our Loved Ones": *Ensign,* May 1986, pp. 20–22.
Chapter 11, "Meeting the Challenges of Economic Stress": *Ensign,* November 1982, pp. 87–90.
Chapter 12, "Comfort and Hope for Families": *Ensign,* November 1984, pp. 54, 59–60.
Chapter 13, "Enriching Our Family Life": *Ensign,* May 1983, pp. 40–42.
Chapter 14, "The Great Imitator": *Ensign,* November 1987, pp. 33–36.
Chapter 15, "Light and Knowledge from Above": *Ensign,* November 1989, pp. 8–11.
Chapter 16, "The Holy Ghost: A Sure Comforter": *Ensign,* May 1989, pp. 31–33.
Chapter 17, "Communion with the Spirit": *Ensign,* May 1990, pp. 12–15.
Chapter 18, "The Supernal Gift of the Atonement": *Ensign,* November 1988, 12–14.

INDEX